*Dickens's
    Hyperrealism*

Dickens's Hyperrealism

JOHN R. REED

THE OHIO STATE UNIVERSITY PRESS • COLUMBUS

Library of Congress Cataloging-in-Publication Data
Reed, John Robert, 1938–
Dickens's hyperrealism / John R. Reed.
   p. cm.
Includes bibliographical references and index.
ISBN 978-0-8142-1138-0 (cloth : alk. paper)—ISBN 978-0-8142-9237-2 (cd)
1. Dickens, Charles, 1812–1870—Criticism and interpretation. 2. Realism in literature.
I. Title.
PR4592.R37R44 2010
823'.8—dc22
                            2010028505

This book is available in the following editions:
Cloth (ISBN 978-0-8142-1138-0)
CD-ROM (ISBN 978-0-8142-9237-2)

Cover design by Jennifer Shoffey Forsythe
Text design by Jennifer Shoffey Forsythe
Type set in Adobe Minion Pro
Printed by Thomson-Shore, Inc.

♾ The paper used in this publication meets the minimum requirements of the American National Standard for Information Sciences—Permanence of Paper for Printed Library Materials. ANSI Z39.48–1992.

9 8 7 6 5 4 3 2 1

CONTENTS

ACKNOWLEDGMENTS

The chapters in this book have appeared elsewhere as individual essays in shorter forms with somewhat different purposes:

- "Dickens on Jacob's Island and the Functions of Literary Descriptions." *Narrative* 7, no. 1 (January 1999): 22–36.
- Susan Lynn Beckwith and John R. Reed. "Impounding the Future: Some Uses of the Present Tense in Dickens and Collins." *Dickens Studies Annual: Essays on Victorian Fiction,* vol. 32, edited by Stanley Friedman, Edward Guiliano, Anne Humpherys, and Michael Timko. New York: AMS Press, 2002. 299–318.
- "Dickens and Naming." *Dickens Studies Annual,* vol. 36, edited by Stanley Friedman, Edward Guiliano, Anne Humpherys, and Michael Timko. New York: AMS Press, 2005. 183–97.
- "The Gentleman in the White Waistcoat: Dickens and Metonymy." *Style* 39, no. 4 (Winter) [late publication]: 412–26.
- "Dickens and Personification." *Dickens Quarterly* 24, no. 1 (March 2007): 3–17.

INTRODUCTION

ven before the term "realism" was brought into general use in England through the writings of G. H. Lewes, there was a general impression of a new kind of writing and Dickens was seen as one of its predecessors.[1] There are certainly elements of realism in the novels of Austen and Scott, but the one excludes a good deal from her fiction, in particular the lower classes, with some exceptions, and the other tends to include some fanciful items in the very structure of his fiction that disallow a clear realist definition.[2] I am thinking of the predictions of doom uttered concerning Edgar Ravenswood in Scott's *The Bride of Lammermoor.* These could have passed as representations of Scottish superstition at the beginning of the eighteenth century if they did not function as part of the novel's design by being fulfilled. Similarly, there is much in Dickens's fiction that certainly appears to be realistic. John Forster records that Dickens himself valued realism above all else in his fiction, but does not elaborate on what that realism meant to Dickens. One need only cite the many urban scenes that vividly evoke the real presence of the city from *Sketches by Boz* on. But I would like to argue that Dickens is actually creating a kind of hyperreality, to borrow a term from Umberto Eco. There is always a touch of exaggeration of the real (and sometimes more than a touch) in Dickens's novels. Donald Hawes puts it this way: "Enter a Dickens novel and you enter a highly charged, multitudinous world, in which realism and imagination are interfused as never before or since" (9). Some critics, such as J. P. Stern, have taken Dickens's abundant and obvious delight in the multitudinousness of the world as an indication that his works fall into the realist camp (1–5), but the very exuberance with which Dickens approaches the world transforms it into something difficult to define as realistic.

Like many other Dickens scholars, I see Dickens as an heir of Romanticism, with an emphasis on the importance of the imagination over simple reason, something in the way that imagination is valued above Facts in *Hard Times*. His inclination is to project the emotions of his characters into the world around them, what Meyer Abrams described in the metaphor of the lamp in *The Mirror and the Lamp*. The tradition of poets such as Wordsworth and Coleridge, who openly described that action of what would come to be known as the Pathetic Fallacy, was continued with a vengeance by such Victorian poets as Tennyson and Browning in poems like "Mariana" and "Childe Roland to the Dark Tower Came." But novelists carried on the tradition as well, Dickens notable among them, and this attention to subjective states to some degree separates such writers from what was to become known as realism.

My approach to realism has mainly to do with narrative method, though I hope I have not ignored the importance of character depiction and other aspects of story telling. But I do not feel obliged to discuss approaches that follow from the tradition of social realism, which has a tendency to confuse content with method. I am not here concerned with how Dickens depicted social institutions such as marriage, or to speculate on whether or not queer theory can be applied to his creation of Sally Brass in *The Old Curiosity Shop*. I prefer to work in the formalist tradition, which has recently been surveyed in its contemporary manifestations by Dario Villanueva in *Theories of Literary Realism*. At times I depend upon the concept of intentionality, a modern version of which Villanueva attributes to Husserl and phenomenology, but I hope that I have provided enough evidence from Dickens's own writings to indicate that he was aware of his own intentions and sought to impose them on his readers, whether they realized this or not. For a framing of what realism means in literature, I am content with Lilian Furst's presentation in *All Is True: The Claims and Strategies of Realist Fiction*.

> On the contrary, realist fiction actively encourages a pretended continuity in the coexistence of the internal realm as an extension of the external. With a canny concealment of any cracks, fictional referents are presented as prolongations of referents known outside the fictions. Although the two frames of reference overlap and share, they do not meet. The internal is adjacent and parallel to the external. So the text projects a new referent, constructing its own reality while simultaneously describing it. This internal reality draws on

a selection of attributes from the actual world, physically and socially, that function as *"reality keys."* The antecedents are related to the text by a process of fictionalization, whereby both historical and geographical data are annexed into the fictive realm as warranties of realism's pretended authenticity. (110)

It is just at the seam where the realist attempts to assert authority and authenticity by disguising the role of the author that Dickens operates, shifting his weight in favor of the author, who slyly or openly establishes authority.

One reason that Dickens has been classed with the realists, as I mentioned above, is his concern for social issues. At least from George Lukács, it has been characteristic to associate the realists with their concern for social improvement, such as alleviating the poverty and working conditions of the lower classes.[3] This approach to realism assumes a direct relationship between text and external reality. As the passage from Furst above suggests, this can never be a firm basis for realism, for realism is a mode of communication distinct from what it discusses, as, it may be argued, are all speech acts. A little later on, I shall discuss how this matter complicates Peter Brooks's treatment of Dickens as a realist. Ioan Williams's 1974 study of the realist novel seems to want to approach realism from a comprehensive point of view, as the following quotation suggests.

Finally, the texture and scope of mid-Victorian novels settle the question. Their solidity and firmness, their humour and breadth of interest in the abundance and variety of human character, and their unprecedented physical, social, and psychological detail, make the term Realist especially appropriate. (x–xi)

But when he finally comes to discuss Dickens, he focuses more on his treatment of character than on the structure and methodology of his novels. One problem is that Williams defines realism in his own particular way. He sees it as manifesting an organic view of human experience which saw imagination and reason as "faculties innate in man, allied to unreflecting consciousness, by which he apprehended total Reality as an undivided whole and himself as one of its parts" (xii). Because he sees Dickens as "the first Victorian writer to conceive and attempt the creation of a vision of contemporary life as organically unified, and to face the technical and structural problems which were involved in this," he must include Dickens among the realists (116).

Williams associates the realist novel with the social novel, so Dickens's depiction of working class life and his clear purpose of effecting social change also links him to realism. And yet, there is much in Williams's argument that hints at another way of reading Dickens and perhaps other Victorian novelists as well. For example, Williams sees the realist novel as part of the Romantic tradition. "Nineteenth century Realist fiction in England is a form of Romantic art, but it differs from Romantic art itself in throwing emphasis on the importance of reproducing the external conditions of life and the material laws" (xii). With regard to Dickens himself, Williams offers a curious view of a general critical attitude in the 70s. "From the modern standpoint, Dickens seems to have escaped from the limitations of Victorian Realism and penetrated to a deeper level of reality" (139). He cites Dickens's interest in abnormal states of consciousness. But while he admits that Dickens was "original and idiosyncratic," he also insists that he was "typical" (139), yet further on he admits that Dickens "was committed to melodramatic and sensational treatment of character, presenting internal processes by external factors" (141). This tension and almost contradiction returns in the ending of his chapter specifically on Dickens.

> It is Dickens's great achievement that dramatic or narrative separateness and conflict can be used in this way, to imply a dimension of life which lies beyond the apparent reality in which his hero-narrator addresses the reader. The nature of this achievement is unique, but the essential principle is common to all Realist fiction—the energy which runs through all men, though distorted by vice, by social circumstances, or by ignorance and weakness, carries meaning and moulds experience itself. (155)

If Dickens's achievement is unique, perhaps it should not so easily be lumped in the category of realism. There is much that is helpful in Williams's discussion of realism, but the contradiction between content and style evident in his treatment of the subject needs to be faced. Hence, I have used the term hyperreality to describe Dickens's self-consciously exaggerated rendering of the world around him. When Eco used the term in *Travels in Hyperreality*, he referred to imitations that were so grotesque that they became mockeries of what they were imitating. In the essay in the collection entitled "Travels in Hyperreality," he takes on such notable American landmarks as Hearst's Castle, Disney World, Forest Lawn, and other such institutions. My alteration of the term is honorific and refers to Dickens's ability to convey a sense of the everyday world while at the same time almost magically transforming it. I don't mean the kind of magic associated with magical realism, but something much more insidious that is rooted in style, not content.

A recent excellent critic runs into similar problems with content and method when including Dickens among the realists. In *Realist Vision*, Peter Brooks admits at the beginning of his chapter on *Hard Times*: "I am of course not sure that it is right to talk about Dickens in the context of realism at all, since so much of Dickens appears as the avoidance or suppression of realism" (40). Brooks's remark reflects the increased sophistication of criticism on Dickens since the 70s, and the outright resistance of some scholars to include Dickens among the realists. But Brooks nonetheless does include him. Remarkably, the text he chooses is *Hard Times,* a novel that, in defending the imagination against a Utilitarian outlook on life, makes abundant use of exaggeration and nonrealist techniques, perhaps most notably in its blatant and highly structured pattern of metaphors. One can understand Brooks's initial doubt about classifying Dickens among the realists, since his perception of *Hard Times* is that it refuses the usual realist task of cataloguing the industrial workplace. In the end, he concludes of the novel that "it is not so much that this novel represents Coketown as that it stands as a counteraction against Coketown, an alternative to it. The novel versus the life of machinery" (52). Perhaps the main reason Brooks did include *Hard Times* in his book is that its subject matter fits so well into one vision of literary realism—the attempt to improve social conditions, especially among the working classes. As I have already suggested, my emphasis is entirely different. Of course Dickens was interested in social improvements, but when it came to his writing, he was also extremely conscious of his craft. And it is on this craft that my emphasis lies.

Not quite so recent, but fully aware of the dilemma of realist classification, Harry E. Shaw feels it necessary to call attention to modern disparagements of realism; he refers to a critical tendency to see realism as a bad alternative to more acceptable modes of narration, and he feels obliged to offer his own definition, which also describes his methodology.

> Nineteenth-century realist fiction can be seen as an attempt to balance procedure and substance, in the concrete modes by which it invites the reader to come to terms with realities, imagined and real. In my own definition of realism I attempt a similar balancing act, by arguing that realism insists that certain mental procedures are needed to make sense of those substantial aspects of the world it selects as significant. A dialectic between substance and procedure is also implicit in my claim that historicist realism involves a movement between positions in and above a given historical moment. (xii)

Shaw has moved away from the materialist basis of earlier critics' approaches to realism, and tends toward a more psychological focus. But he is fully aware of the various ways in which modern criticism has defined and interpreted realism, and his first chapter is a handy survey of some notable positions on the subject.

J. Jeffrey Franklin goes further than Shaw in suggesting that Victorian realists were not interested in mirroring nature, but concerned with the true as distinguished from the real (25).[4] He likens them to postmodern writers, for "they perform a revised version of society into existence by both thematically representing and formally enacting a reality that is similar to but 'truer' than social reality" (30). Franklin emphasizes the important role of play, both as a subject and as a textual manner in the writers he examines. He touches only briefly upon Dickens, but concludes his study with an interesting suggestion as far as genre studies are concerned.

> Even so, perhaps it is time to expand and redefine the concept of realism to encompass not only Charles Dickens's *Our Mutual Friend* and Victor Hugo's *The Hunchback of Notre Dame*, for example, but also James Joyce's *Ulysses* and Toni Morrison's *Beloved*. (204)

This solution seems to me to make realism such a diluted term that it can be applied to all sorts of literature. The inclusion of such an obviously Modernist work as *Ulysses* highlights the problem. I would rather employ a different term, and hyperreality seems a good one, to call attention to the theatricality of Dickens's approach. But he is doing more than just borrowing techniques from the stage; he is placing himself in the position of producer and stage manager as well. Most critics will admit that Dickens borrowed a good deal from the theater and that he enjoyed a certain amount of melodrama in his novels. In a recent collection, John Glavin puts it this way:

> Pretty much everyone agrees Dickens's fiction is spectacular. I'm going to literalize that claim to say that in an era of Spectacular Theatre Dickens wrote a comparably Spectacular Fiction, where Spectacular, on both stage and page, meant something like realism eradicated. (*Cambridge Companion* 190)

My approach to Dickens and realism involves a balancing act rather different from Shaw's. I have in mind Roland Barthes's useful distinction between readerly and writerly texts. In the former, the reader is granted a good deal of interpretive freedom, in the latter, the author seeks to maintain authority. I shall argue that Dickens was fully aware of these positions, though he might not have been able to offer critical interpretations of them. What Dickens tried to do from rather early in his career was to give his audience the impression that they were reading readerly texts, while, in fact, he was writing writerly texts.[5] In the later part of his career he took to pointing out either overtly or through such things as plot devices or metaphorical patterns, his domination of his own stories. Several of the late novels actually have to be reread to be fully grasped, with *Our Mutual Friend* perhaps being the outstanding example.

However, by way of illustration, I would like to juxtapose a passage from *Dombey and Son* in the middle of Dickens's career, with one from his contemporary Mrs. Gaskell's *Sylvia's Lovers,* a novel that fits two narrative descriptions, for it is, I believe a good example of realism in the more limited genre of the domestic novel.[6] The first is a description of Carker the manager's home. Dickens has already given an objective description of the neat and convenient nature of the exterior and to some degree the interior of the bachelor's house at the beginning of chapter 33. Then he proceeds:

> And yet, amidst this opulence of comfort, there is something in the general air that is not well. Is it that the carpets and the cushions are too soft and noiseless, so that those who move or repose among them seem to act by stealth? Is it that the prints and pictures do not commemorate great thoughts or deeds, or render nature in the poetry of landscape, hall, or hut, but are of one voluptuous cast—mere shows of form and colour—and no more? Is it that the books have all their gold outside, and that the titles of the greater part qualify them to be companions of the prints and titles of the pictures? Is it that the completeness and the beauty of the place is here and there belied by an affectation of humility, in some unimportant and inexpensive regard, which is as false as the face of the too truly painted portrait hanging yonder, or its original at breakfast in his easy chair below it? Or is it that, with the daily breath of that original and master of all here, there issues forth some subtle portion of himself, which gives a vague expression of himself to everything about him! (471–72)

Unlike the objective narrator of realism, Dickens's narrator emphasizes his presence by way of a series of rhetorical questions, which, while implicating the reader in the interpretation of the catalogue, nonetheless prevents him from taking charge of that interpretation himself. His description is not intended to mirror the world. The first paragraph did that to some degree. He is here offering an imaginatively altered "real" world by attributing moral values to it through such loaded words as "stealth," "voluptuous," and "false." Moreover, this passage explicitly states the notion behind Dickens's repeated method throughout his work, by suggesting that Carker's character permeates the area and objects around him, just as Dickens cloaks his narratives in specific moral fabrics, largely the projections of the characters' traits, or of the narrator's own moods. In many cases these projections are connected by repetitions of one kind or another, often of patterns of imagery. In short, Dickens's narrator not only dominates the "picture" he is presenting, but also weaves it into the larger structure of the narrative as a whole. In later works this technique becomes more subtle, but here he is letting the audience see the magician's sleight of hand.

The passage from *Sylvia's Lovers* is typical of Gaskell and of realism.

> Foster's shop was the shop of Monkshaven. It was kept by two Quaker brothers, who were now old men; and their father had kept it before them; probably his father before that. People remembered it as an old-fashioned dwelling-house, with a sort of supplementary shop with unglazed windows projecting from the lower story. These openings had long been filled with panes of glass that at the present day would be accounted very small, but which seventy years ago were much admired for their size. I can best make you understand the appearance of the place by bidding you think of the long openings in a butcher's shop, and then to fill them up in your imagination with panes about eight inches by six, in a heavy wooden frame. There was one of these windows on each side the door-place, which was kept partially closed through the day by a low gate about a yard high. Half the shop was appropriated to grocery; the other half to drapery, and a little mercery. (22)

There is no attempt to characterize the owners of the shop by its contents. Although the narrator intrudes herself, it is only to help the reader picture the limited nature of the shop's window by a comparison with windows of her own day. The shop is inserted into an historical frame. Certainly at this point in the novel there is no need for us to know that the proprietors are Quakers, so this information has the superfluous feel so characteristic of realist description. The narrator might speculate (probably the grandfather of the current owners owned the shop too), but offers no moral assessments. We are given a scene to evaluate and the narrator does not coerce us, as Dickens's narrator does, by emphasizing Carker's preference for the voluptuous—something stressed throughout the text by various means, including the association of Carker with cats.

The preceding comments discuss recent critical attitudes regarding literary realism in general and Dickens in particular. But Dickens has been something of a problem from his own day. George H. Ford pointed out some time ago that as early as 1852, David Masson contrasted Dickens and Thackeray, putting the former in the category of ideal novelists and the latter in that of real novelist; to Masson, Dickens was poetic, though he did not necessarily mean this as a high compliment (Ford 116). For George Henry Lewes, Dickens did not live up to the standards of realism, which Lewes equated with the faithful representation of everyday existence, because his writings were hallucinatory (Ford 149ff). Some clue to Dickens's attitude can be found in his diatribe against Mr. Barlow, the stern teacher in the children's book *Sandford and Merton,* in "Mr. Barlow" in *The Uncommercial Traveller.* Dickens dislikes the humorless Mr. Barlow because he represents a heavily didactical approach to fiction. As a child, Dickens felt he was an imposition, wholly unlike the story telling that he preferred. Dickens writes: "The incompatibility of Mr. Barlow with all other portions of my young life but himself, the adamantine inadaptability of the man to my favorite fancies and amusements is the thing for which I hate him most. What right had he to bore his way into my Arabian Nights?" (339). This says it all. Dickens wanted some of the magic of the *Arabian Nights* wedded to the commonplaceness of the world around him, the romantic side of everyday things, as he put it himself. The program of realism accurately to reflect the world as it is might have appeared is too like the Utilitarian outlook excoriated in *Hard Times* (where the *Arabian Nights* is used effectively as a critical weapon) for Dickens to be sympathetic.

Dickens seems to have been misunderstood even by those who thoroughly enjoyed his novels. John Forster observed that what mattered to Dickens was that he gave a true impression of the world as it is, an attitude that can be confused with the realist endeavor (Ford 132). But he often commented on the truth as a moral truth. Hence, while he sought to render the material world in a factual manner, he also sought to enhance it for the improvement of his readers. His famous comment in the introduction to *Bleak House* that he wished to convey the romantic side of everyday life sums up this attitude.

One useful way of looking at Dickens's fiction was proposed some while ago by Edward Eigner in *The Metaphysical Novel in England and America: Dickens, Bulwer, Hawthorne, Melville* (1978). Eigner borrows the term "metaphysical novel" from Bulwer. In Bulwer in particular such novels were a "mixture of allegory and the matter-of-fact" (5). It was necessary to depict the material world as it was in order to subject it to a grand intellectual or moral design. "They had to present the experiential world view as compellingly as possible before they could even generate the energy to contradict it with the opposite epistemic method" (181). These novels were characterized by premeditation; they had a scheme to which all else was subordinate. Thus, unlike the realist novel, character development was not important; characters served the overall design of the narrative. Eigner notes that "the metaphysical novelist does not proceed from ignorance, as the realist does, but from preconceived vision or truth" (64). Character development is the signature of nineteenth-century realist fiction; it is a main avenue for the pursuit of truth. But Eigner points out that "the metaphysical novelists recognized the idealized or simplified character as an injunction from German romantic aesthetics, but also as the heritage of the major forms of narrative which had come down to them: epic, romance, and satire" (71). The narrator of the metaphysical novel also tended to be intrusive in a way that most realists avoided. This forwardness of the narrator "offered an advantage to the metaphysical novelist, for if the reader could be forced to observe the creative process itself, not simply be permitted to watch the creation, he might become a participant in the vision rather than merely a spectator" (64–65). As I shall suggest in what follows, Dickens always wanted his readers to appreciate the craft with which he constructed his narratives, as his prefaces indicate.

I shall not be discussing all of Dickens's fiction. I shall, for example, have nothing to say about the historical novels *Barnaby Rudge* and *A Tale of Two Cities*. My discussions shall be concerned more with Dickens's narrative method than with his subject matter or his moral objectives, both of which were certainly important to him.

CHAPTER 1

Description¹

$\mathcal{D}$ escriptive detail is surely a characteristic of realist fiction, sometimes even to the point of offending some readers' sensibilities. There can be no doubt that Dickens was capable of extraordinary descriptive power, but that feature alone would not put him in the realist camp. In this chapter, focusing largely on *Oliver Twist*, I shall examine how, early in his career, Dickens had already developed a characteristic function for his descriptions.

Modern readers of *Oliver Twist* (1838), though powerfully moved by its culminating scenes of Bill Sikes's flight from the mob and death by accidental hanging from a house on Jacob's Island, might be little inclined to pay much attention to the setting of these events. They may find the precise poetic justice the narrative enacts a little hard to swallow, but are not likely to raise the kind of objections that Sir Peter Laurie did when he claimed that there was no such place as Jacob's Island in London, a place he said "ONLY existed in a work of fiction written by Mr. Charles Dickens".² Sir Peter was obviously not reading for the plot, but for an accurate representation of the world he believed he knew. Scholars and anyone who has read Dickens's preface to the first Cheap Edition of *Oliver Twist* will recall that Dickens insisted upon the real existence of Jacob's Island, an assertion that has led some scholars to deplore Dickens's attempt to transform his moral fable into a realistic depiction of nineteenth-century urban life.[3] For the literal-minded of Dickens's day, the situation should have been simple. Draw a map and let them visit Jacob's Island if it exists in reality. Less literal-minded readers might acknowledge that a representation of a real *condition* does not have to be a representation of a real *place*.[4] The fact that there is no place *named* Jacob's Island does not mean that its *type* does not exist, with its squalid population, narrow streets, decrepit houses, and mud. Dickens's assertion that Jacob's Island did exist, however, seems to be a claim on his part that his story is realistic, not merely fanciful. But I shall try to show that that was not his purpose. This early in his career, he knew what he wanted to achieve with his descriptions.

In what follows, I examine description of real places in fictional texts, concentrating on the example of Jacob's Island in *Oliver Twist*. Description has long been undervalued as a narrative device. This chapter is an attempt to refocus attention upon the narrative contributions description can make. Of course there are many types of description, from the concrete efforts at "realism" in Arnold Bennett's *Anna of the Five Towns* to the striking imaginary descriptions in H. G. Wells's *The Time Machine*. These descriptions serve different ends and can carry different ideological messages and achieve different esthetic purposes. Later, I shall compare the role of descriptions of place in Thomas Hardy and Emily Brontë with Dickens's, especially in *Oliver Twist*, but my main intention here is to show how one form of description— that of real places—can serve as a powerful vehicle of ideological purpose precisely because it occurs in a fictional text. Dickens, I argue, is successful in this way because he is able to make such description operate diegetically and also extradiegetically by imbedding this almost matter-of-fact description in a compelling moral fable—what today we might call a kind of hyper-reality. In a way it is the opposite of the rhetorical device of enlivening the exposition of a sermon by including an amusing though instructive exemplum.

In a recent study of nineteenth-century literature and culture entitled *Novel Possibilities,* Joseph W. Childers—struggling against what he sees as a tide of recent theoretical arguments that suggest literary works make no real difference, but merely engage in an intertextual discourse confined to the world of texts—contends that fiction not only relates to its social condition, but that it has agency and can participate in the transformation of that condition.[5] Charles Dickens certainly believed that his writings could and did contribute to changes in the social conditions of his time, not least his descriptions of the workhouse and of the slum conditions of Jacob's Island in *Oliver Twist*. Dickens's response to Sir Peter Laurie's charge that Jacob's Island appeared in Dickens's novel and was therefore imaginary was that Sir Peter Laurie himself had appeared in a book some years before (Dickens had reason to know, since it was he who represented the alderman in his Christmas book *The Chimes*) and therefore Laurie, too, must be imaginary (384). This response would, of course, seem facetious to a literary critic of the present day, since she or he would immediately reply that we are talking here about representation. Of course Dickens knew that too, but he also believed that he could persuade his readers to actual changes in their lives through the power of his representations. Not only did he not believe that the author was dead, he believed that the true author never died.[6] And he believed that the true author had genuine intentions to carry out and should control his narrative in such a way that they had their intended effect.

What status does the description of a real place have in a fictional narrative? How do we treat the register of "imaginary" characters, events, and locations, as opposed to the register of a "real" place? A simple response to the question is that the London of *Oliver Twist* is not a real place. It, too, is a representation. Never mind that Dickens names places that have real existence—St. Paul's Cathedral, the Old Bailey, Newgate prison; these, too, are simply markers and bear no more than a trace of the actual places. Never mind also that Dickens is so particular about the route that Bill Sikes and Oliver take on their way to burgle the Maylie household or the equally particular route that Bill Sikes pursues after his murder of Nancy. These excursions might have an internal significance to Dickens's narrative, but do they matter in relationship to the real environs of London? Dickens himself seems to suggest that they do not by making the first excursion problematic through the episode of the mysterious house that Oliver (incorrectly?) identifies, and the second through its phantasmal qualities. These interpretations of described places are complicated by the interference of the characters' psychic states. That is not the case with the description of Jacob's Island, which comes to us directly from the narrative voice.[7] I do not here wish to reanimate the real/imaginary binary in the light of deconstructive and other recent theoretical approaches, but more modestly to call attention to peculiar creases in the fabric of interpretation when we try to distinguish how certain forms of description operate in fiction and what tools might be helpful to deal with them.[8]

In *Fiction and Diction*, Gérard Genette concludes that "Except for the fictionality of their context, the speech acts of fictional characters, whether the fiction is dramatic or narrative, are authentic acts, fully endowed with the locutionary characteristics of such acts, with their 'point' and their illocutionary force, and with their potential perlocutionary effects, intended or not" (33). He further concludes that there is therefore no reason why authors (his example is Tolstoy) cannot include maxims and descriptive utterances in their fictions. More explicitly, he declares that "utterances of the historical or geographical type . . . are not necessarily deprived of their truth value by being inserted into a fictional context and subordinated to fictional ends" (49).

If expressions of opinion by fictional characters are acceptable as authentic speech acts and "true" descriptions of place are allowable by narrators of novels, then in what way do they differ from a traveler's or autobiographer's expressions of opinion or "true" accounts of the places he or she has seen? When, for example, A. W. Kinglake in *Eothen* describes the exotic locations of the Middle East, are his descriptions more authentic than those that might appear in a novel, or that might appear in a travel book written by a novelist, as in Thackeray's *From Cornhill to Cairo*? Both factual and fictive description is filtered through individual subjectivity, and, as Edward Said has made clear in *Orientalism*, whole cultures can develop screens for what they describe; hence any European might be inclined to distort the Middle Eastern object of his description because of his cultural preconceptions about the Orient.

Oliver Twist does not involve the kind of exoticism that Said explores. Here we are talking about Londoners looking at and reporting the London of their own day. Nonetheless, we must still acknowledge that observers bring to the sights they see certain preconceptions about race, class, and even geographical location. A poor Irishman might see the neighborhood of Bermondsey in 1838 very differently from an Englishman of the middle or upper classes. Certain London neighborhoods were presumed by middle-class citizens to have nefarious or unattractive characters, for example, Seven Dials, Snow Hill, and Whitechapel. Later in this chapter I shall suggest that it is precisely against such prescripting of place that fictional description can work in a way that it cannot in "true" reportage because fictional description is installed in an imaginary narrative, which has its own generative force.

But for now let us return to the basic question: what role does the description of a real location play when it appears in a work of fiction?[9] More specifically, how does Dickens's description of an urban slum within a work of fiction operate in the imaginary not only of his own day, but in those of subsequent historical periods? Raymond Williams approaches this subject broadly in *The Country and the City*. To begin with, he notes that London was unusual as great cities of the nineteenth century went. Its "miscellaneity and randomness," he says, "in the end embodied a system: a negative system of indifference; a positive system of differentiation, in law, power and financial control. But the characteristic of London—capital city of a complex national and overseas economy and society—was that this was not, in any simple way, physically apparent" (154). Dickens perceived this peculiarity and captured it not in his actual descriptions of place, but in an innovative novelistic maneuver.

Dickens's creation of a new kind of novel—a creative achievement which had many false starts, many lapses, but in the end was decisive—can be directly related to what we must see as this double condition: the random and the systematic, the visible and the obscured, which is the true significance of the city, and especially at this period of the capital city, as a dominant social form.

Dickens's ultimate vision of London is then not to be illustrated by topography or local instance. It lies in the form of his novels: in their kind of narrative, in their method of characterisation, in their genius for typification. (154)

For Dickens, Williams adds, "[t]he city is shown as at once a social fact and a human landscape" (158). But, keen and helpful as this perception is, it does not resolve our issue. Williams implies that the specific description of place is relatively insignificant in Dickens's representation of London and that it is the larger form of the novel that provides a conceptual equivalent of the city. I argue that the specific descriptions of real places remain highly charged ideological and representational nodes. Dickens could make place work effectively as the setting for dramatic action, thereby giving location a force that carried over from the diegetic or narrative world into the nonfictional, extradiegetic world. But his rendering of real places did not have the realistic novel's ambition of transparency; rather, he wished his artfulness to be obvious in a manner essentially unwelcome to realism.

To begin with, it is important to realize that Jacob's Island *did* exist and not merely in the mind of Charles Dickens. It even appeared in contemporary maps of the city. So the alderman of real London, Sir Peter Laurie, did not know his city as well as did the great fabler Charles Dickens. In fact, the very year that Sir Peter made his remarks about Jacob's Island, Henry Mayhew was commissioned by the registrar general to make a report on that location, which was published in the *Morning Chronicle* on 24 September 1849. Anne Humpherys writes: "The place had hardly changed since Dickens's famous exposé: Mayhew found the same rotting houses and the same filthy ditch" (16). Humpherys suggests that the whole series that became *London Labour and London Poor* grew out of this report. Drawing upon his own experiences and Mayhew's researches, Charles Kingsley offered a powerful picture of Jacob's Island in *Alton Locke* (1850), a novel that had considerable social impact. Not only, then, was Jacob's Island a real place, but it became established in fictional and nonfictional texts as a representative place—a stereotypical urban slum.[10]

When you get right down to it, Dickens's description of Jacob's Island is brief and not very particularized. After a paragraph describing the unsightly approaches to the place, Dickens's narrator arrives at Jacob's Island, first describing Folly Ditch, which surrounds it, before becoming more specific.

> Crazy wooden galleries common to the backs of half-a-dozen houses, with holes from which to look upon the slime beneath; windows, broken and patched: with poles thrust out, on which to dry the linen that is never there; rooms so small, so filthy, so confined, that the air would seem too tainted even for the dirt and squalor which they shelter; wooden chambers thrusting themselves out above the mud, and threatening to fall into it—as some have done; dirt-besmeared walls and decaying foundations; every repulsive lineament of poverty, every loathsome indication of filth, rot, garbage; all these ornament the banks of Folly Ditch.
>
> In Jacob's Island, the warehouses are roofless and empty; the walls are crumbling down; the windows are windows no more; the doors are falling into the streets; the chimneys are blackened, but they yield no smoke. Thirty or forty years ago, before losses and chancery suits came upon it, it was a thriving place; but now it is a desolate island indeed. The houses have no owners; they are broken open, and entered upon by those who have the courage; and there they live and there they die. They must have powerful motives for a secret residence, or be reduced to a destitute condition indeed, who seek a refuge in Jacob's Island. (300)

And this is the whole of the description. It could be argued that much of the power of the description relies on what is not there: the linen, the smoke, the details of the chancery suits, and the motives for residing at Jacob's Island. Also, the extension of description to social commentary strengthens the passage. Anne Humpherys compares Dickens's text with Mayhew's, which is far more detailed, including repulsive colors. She concludes that Dickens's more general description gains its superior effect because of the personification it employs and because it thereby becomes representative of all slums in London (192). Perhaps it is this trait that makes Dickens's description so memorable. But, in fact, there is very little that could be called personification in this famous passage. Indeed, the language, though it incorporates details, such as the poles thrust out for the drying of linen, the "besmeared walls and decaying foundations," and the blackened chimneys that "yield no smoke," is remarkably restrained. There is certainly a judgmental tone in the narrative voice, as the adjectives and nouns indicate—crazy, slime, filthy, squalor, filth, rot, garbage. Yet this description is nothing like the startlingly animated description of the factories at Coketown in *Hard Times*, where the extreme metaphoricity calls attention to itself, producing memorable images while not providing many actual details about the buildings and grounds.

The description of Jacob's Island is less spectacular, closer to reportage, and perhaps because less theatrical, more credible.

Besides the possible effect of personification, there is another reason that Dickens's description is more forceful than the many nonfictional descriptions of slum conditions—and there were many written at the time of *Oliver Twist* and later. Dickens's description is embedded in a compelling narrative with striking characters who act out their deeds in the settings, both real and fictional, that Dickens chose to describe. The fictional narrative becomes the energizing vehicle that carries and lends force to the description of the real place that then transfers that energy to the real world by way of the reader's reception of it. But why is this narrative more powerful and lasting than nonfictional narratives containing nonfictional descriptions of similar places?

Raymond Williams takes for granted in his estimate of Dickens's treatment of London something that has to be rediscovered by others. In *Resisting Novels,* Lennard J. Davis instructs us that "[n]ovels do not depict life, they depict life as it is represented by ideology" (24). The purpose of a highly mimetic fiction is "to help humans adapt to the fragmentation and isolation of the modern world" (12). The danger is that we might forget the ideological character of novels and accept them as natural embodiments of common sense. Description of place is part of a larger system of meaning. In novels written in the nineteenth century, landscapes, and more particularly cityscapes, evoke the sense of property and hence a symbolic system associated with money and market values. Davis says that "Dickens made or remade London, particularly for his reforming purposes. He is rarely writing about a universal London, but writing about a London with contemporary problems and proposed solutions" (89). Dickens's descriptions thus arise from a reforming intention and embody an appropriate ideology. When he describes the "real" London, he is incorporating it in a system of values which he promotes. His aggressively fictional narrative nonetheless refers back to the "real" world. Who would care about the slum dwellers in daily life? But we *know* the Bill Sikes who dies in their loathsome quarters. By peopling London with his imaginary characters, Dickens makes it more real than a journalist, obliged to confine himself to the "truth," might do.

It has long been appreciated that the creation of character is a device that seduces readers into the fictive world. Davis writes that "ideologically speaking . . . character gives readers faith that personality is first, understandable and, second, capable of rational change" (119). Catherine Gallagher, drawing upon a history of critical insight, notes that "[e]ighteenth-century readers identified with the characters in novels because of the characters' fictiveness and not in spite of it. Moreover, these readers had to be taught how to read fiction, and as they learned this skill (it did not come naturally), new emotional dispositions were created." Indeed, Gallagher goes on to note that each generation of writers felt compelled to reform the genre "by encouraging an affective pulsation between identification with fictional characters and withdrawal from them" (xvii). But if characterization is an obvious way to blur the distinction between the fictive and the real world, description is its almost invisible co-agent. Readers of fiction had to be taught how to read description as well as character with similar results. Being like us, characters are easy to judge on the basis of how they behave. Unlike us, streets, buildings, and rivers do not "behave" and therefore cannot be "judged" in any scheme of morals. But they can nonetheless *embody* such judgments and they do this best when they are embedded in imaginary narratives where certain moral values are asserted. Characterization, and even description of character, when charged with stereotypical details (as in those employing terms from phrenology or physiognomy) can bear a heavy ideological weight. So can description of place, though generally less obviously.

Description serves many different purposes in fiction, and there is a great diversity in the relationship between "real" places and those represented in fiction. The opening of H. G. Wells's *The Island of Dr. Moreau* gives specific longitudinal and latitudinal directions for the point in the Pacific Ocean where the fictional island is located, but no one since the days of *Gulliver's Travels* would suppose that this site, though existing in the real world, has any genuine connection with the fictional world of Wells's novel except that it indicates a location remote and tropical which is consistent with Wells's story.[11]

Ordinarily, fictional descriptions call attention to their fictiveness and there are innumerable ways that they can do this. A novel set in the remote future assumes a setting inevitably different in many ways from any real place in the present. Some novels assign fictional names to places and give them generic descriptions. Conrad's eastern novels, for example, only ask you to accept their tropicality, not their *topicality*. And then there is the remarkable example of Italo Calvino's *Invisible Cities*, where the cities that Marco Polo describes for Genghis Kahn—sometimes in words, sometimes in symbols—are projections of subjective states: dreams, anxieties, desires. Even real places can acquire a fictive quality by being focalized through the mood of a character, as José Manuel Lopes shows with Zola's treatment of Paris in *Une Page d'amour* (1878).[12]

All descriptions, as ingredients of novels, bear some ideological weight. But some are more intimately connected to moral judgment than others. Thomas Hardy is credited with "creating" the fictional world of Wessex, though readers in his day and ours have understood that his descriptions adhere faithfully to real locations in Dorset, Devon, Somerset, and Wiltshire.

Scholarly editions of his novels call attention to the fact that Melchester is "really" Salisbury, Casterbridge is "really" Dorchester, Christchurch is "really" Oxford, and so on. Academic and other tours are arranged every year to visit the real settings of Hardy's novels, though most of the urban settings are greatly changed, if the landscape remains generally the same. But, though everyone admits the existence of real places—urban and rural—that correspond to the places described in Hardy's novels, are these "fictional" descriptions of the same order as Dickens's description of Jacob's Island? We can draw maps of Wessex and pinpoint the various places that Hardy incorporated in his novels. And we can correctly declare that Hardy's descriptions are often extremely vivid, but what fictional purpose do these descriptions serve? Do Hardy's descriptions generally make claims that extend beyond the novels in which they occur? I suggest that, for the most part, Hardy's descriptions of place serve almost exclusively diegetic ends. They may reveal characters' moods, symbolize themes, and so forth, but they rarely aim to escape the constraints of the narrative to operate directly upon an audience for other than esthetic reasons. A case might be made for Christchurch in *Jude the Obscure* as an exception, but I won't make it.

Emily Brontë's *Wuthering Heights* offers another example. Much writing about the Brontës emphasizes the Yorkshire setting in which they grew up. *Wuthering Heights,* in particular, is said to incorporate the bleak countryside near Haworth. The setting of *Wuthering Heights* certainly has thematic and atmospheric importance in the novel, though descriptions of terrain are generally unspecific. Yet so strong is the impulse to convert imaginary places into real ones, or at least into realizable forms, that J. Frank Goodridge took the trouble in his essay "The Circumambient Universe" to provide a detailed map of the countryside surrounding and including Wuthering Heights and Thrushcross Grange. This map does not resemble the countryside near Haworth in any detail and therefore does not relate directly to Brontë's biography. What is the function of the map, then, as it relates to Brontë's novel? Since place in the novel is largely symbolic or representative, the spatial layout of the various important loci does not seem significant. The ideology of Brontë's novel does not have the same designs upon its audience that Dickens's does. I do not here refer to a conscious ideology, but merely the ideology inhering in the text. The literal "mapping" of *Wuthering Heights'* setting does not enhance, but detracts from the quality of the narrative because the function of place in the novel is to mirror internal states, not to call attention to external conditions.[13] It is almost perverse to embody as real a place that draws its power from its imaginary character. The fictional place is truer than any representation of it can be. The ultimate abuse in this direction may be the opposite of the Jacob's Island controversy—the stipulation of the location in modern London of the original *Old Curiosity Shop* from Dickens's novel of the same name. In this case, a claim is proffered (though not very seriously) that an entirely imaginary place has a real location.[14]

There are notable differences in the way description of place functions in, say, Hardy's *Jude*, Brontë's *Heights*, and Dickens's *Twist*. In *Jude*, the novel's design is crucial and the descriptions of Christchurch, though they may refer to the actual Oxford, serve that design. Although there are implicit judgments about social inequity in these passages, there is no move by the narrator to traverse the gap between diegetic and extradiegetic worlds. Whatever ideological work is done here is subtle, not targeted. Moreover, these descriptions are problematic in another way because they are focalized to a great extent through Jude's consciousness. Jude's picture of Christchurch is false and the narrator knows it. The "real" place of Oxford, then, accommodates the function of the fictional character. This is even more the case in *Wuthering Heights*, where descriptions of place do not evoke a real place, such as Haworth, but serve symbolic purposes. Brontë's narrative seems purposely to exclude and even obscure any extradiegetic connection. Description is hermetically sealed within the diegesis and even within the imbedded narrative, since Lockwood, as he narrates his own experience and what he has heard from Nelly Dean, does not seem to perceive the symbolic nature of the matter he conveys. By contrast, though Dickens's description of the real named place of Jacob's Island serves the design of the novel, the reliable, even authoritative, narrative voice also aims beyond the limits of the diegesis to the extradiegetic world in which the represented Jacob's Island really exists. Crucial to this act is the authorial intention to address an audience that is capable of receiving the conscious ideological message as both diegetic and extradiegetic. Assumed in this narrative gesture is a conviction that the discourse of fiction "translates" to the real world. It is at moments like this that Dickens's capacity to create a writerly and a readerly text at the same time becomes evident. He wishes to control the import of his text, but he also wants his readers to participate inventively in it. This is something that realist fiction avoids.

The whole question of the effect of descriptions of real places in fiction is contained within the larger question of the relationship between fictional and nonfictional discourse. The question has received increased attention in the last couple of decades. John R. Searle claims: "There is no textual property, syntactical or semantic, that will identify a text as a work of fiction. What makes it a work of fiction is, so to speak, the illocutionary stance that the author takes toward it, and that stance is a matter of the complex illocutionary intentions that the author has when he writes or otherwise composes it" (*Expression* 65–66).[15] The author of fictional texts pretends to use illocutionary acts and therefore suspends the normal rules governing texts. This view and others involved in the debate about fictional and nonfictional texts are surveyed by Richard Rorty in "Is There a Problem about Fictional Discourse?" The whole dispute, he suggests, crystallizes in the question "what, if anything, turns on the difference between being 'really there' and being 'made up'? For what purpose is a convenient fiction as good as reality?" (110). Starting with Bertrand Russell and working forward to Searle, Donnellan, and others, Rorty then traces the problem back to Parmenides and the distinction between the discourse of science and the discourse of poetry. But Rorty moves away from the specific discussion of fiction to the broader issue of what we can tell the truth about, and concludes with a position sympathetic to a physicalist semantic which he condenses in the proposition "whatever is referred to must be the sort of object which we have to talk about in order to give the Ideal Causal Explanation of our saying what we say" (134). In Parmenidian terms, this is a first-rate discourse ("scientific" discourse that deals with logic, proofs, demonstrations, etc.). This discourse is beneficial to second-rate discourse ("literary" discourse that deals with rhetoric, value judgment, aesthetic effect, etc.) because it provides a foil against which irony and reflexive writing can take place. Thus for Rorty, only first-rate discourses can convey truths.

What Rorty seems to overlook is that what he calls scientific or first-rate discourses have a tendency to come into and go out of fashion. Thomas Kuhn has demonstrated how scientific paradigms supersede one another, calling up new forms of language to articulate them. Often the scientific languages themselves are based upon hidden or even obvious metaphors and other tropes. We need only glance at the anthropological assumptions of the nineteenth century that passed as scientific fact to appreciate how unsteadily they rested upon master narratives of Providence, Progress, and race or gender hierarchies.

The debate about the relative standings of fictional and nonfictional texts remains unresolved, leaving the question of description of real places in fiction texts still open, since Searle, for one, is willing to admit that "[a] work of fiction need not consist entirely of, and in general will not consist entirely of, fictional discourse" (*Expression* 74). He thus prepares for Genette's remark, quoted earlier, that real descriptions can legitimately appear in fictional texts. The whole issue is complicated by the fact that nonfictional narratives have always felt free to employ techniques associated with fiction, including figurative language, prolepsis and analepsis, focalization, imagined dialogue, characterization, and so forth. The point is that from news reporting to historical representation to philosophical dispute, first-rate discourse has availed itself of methods characteristically associated with second-rate discourse (scientific discourse, for example, is heavily dependent upon metaphor). Both modes of discourse share the same resources of language, both are circumscribed in what they can achieve by the limitations of language.

Assertions about the death of the author and the hermetic intertextuality of literature obscure the fact that a great many major literary texts continue to evoke similar patterns of response in widely different audiences. Of course any artifact, including a fictional narrative, may be misinterpreted. A person from a very different culture might well wonder what function a toilet stool serves in the United States. But once the context becomes clear, most "readers" quickly figure out the semiotics of bathrooms, street signs, and narrative conventions. Modern American teenagers may know nothing about the strict class structure of nineteenth-century England, but they soon grasp its general significance in narratives depicting Victorian society.

A short while back, Wolfgang Iser reopened an old issue by examining in detail what he calls "the imaginary." In effect, he proposes that underlying all human intellectual activity is our power to conceive, in an "as if" manner, what does not yet exist. From this point of view, first-rate discourse itself depends upon a mental gesture akin to fiction making. What, after all, is a scientific hypothesis but a *fabula* to be elaborated as *sujet*? The ability to fictionalize thus becomes a rudimentary and essential human trait. As Iser puts it, "[t]he state of being above and outside oneself is not merely a transitory phase but is a fundamental characteristic of humanity." He adds that "Hans-Georg Gadamer considers this state to be a major achievement of mankind" (84). This power has consequences for human identity as well. "With literary fictionality, the process of stepping out of and above oneself always retains what has been overstepped, and in this form of doubling we are present to ourselves as our own differential." But though fiction seems to operate as a frame of reference for self-fashioning, it actually does the opposite. "Because it indicates that human beings cannot be present to themselves, literary fictionality involves the condition of being creative right through to our dreams without ever allowing us to coincide with ourselves through what we create. What we do create is the conceivability of this basic disposition, and as this eludes our grasp, fictionality turns also into a judgment that human beings make about themselves" (86).

Iser argues that literary fictions (unlike nonliterary fictions such as "the founding of institutions, societies, and world pictures") reveal their fictionality. They contain large numbers of identifiable items from the outside world, as well as from previous literature, that "are now marked as being fictionalized. Thus the incorporated 'real' world is, so to speak, placed in brackets to indicate that it is not something given but is merely to be understood as if it were given. . . . Reality, then, may be reproduced to be outstripped, as is indicated by its being bracketed" (12–13). This account satisfies situations that involve fictional descriptions such as those in Hardy and Brontë, who, I would argue, aspire more toward the realist end of the fictional spectrum than Dickens does. But I am arguing that the example from *Oliver Twist* functions in a different manner under a different intentionality. Just as the political conversations in Disraeli's *Coningsby* are meant to operate in the real world in precisely the way they do in the novel, so Dickens's description of Jacob's Island, though it serves the design of the novel, is meant to replicate, not merely double, the real place, but it does so in a peculiar manner that has to do with the special place of description in narrative.

In "Rhetorical Status of the Descriptive," Phillipe Hamon relates how rhetoricians historically have distrusted description. He concludes that "description might be that place in the text where the generative power of language might show itself most clearly and as quite unmanageable" (25). Hamon also says that description is often "the place in the text where the 'work' of the author is most visibly manifest" (21). Description thus becomes the textual site where intentionality might be most clearly isolated. It is the almost invisible reservoir of ideology that flows openly but muddied in dialogue and story.

Iser indicates that literary fictions, because of their doubling of reality and their relations to other texts, are always semantically unstable. Description is one of the potentially most unstable narrative elements since there need be no limit to its proliferation. I would like to suggest that the potency of Dickens's description of Jacob's Island derives largely from the fact that this potentially eruptive passage, occurring when closure of the narrative (and, as Iser would say, the imaginative game) is imminent, does not erupt as it might into a torrent of details about the slum conditions of Jacob's Island, but exploits its own instability through an intensifying constraint. Dickens knew that his middle-class audience accepted certain London neighborhoods as prescripted slums. They understood, at least theoretically, what constituted a slum. By not elaborating his description in the way Mayhew did, or a realist novelist might do, Dickens stimulated his audience to fill in the details. The reader reads the description as a setting for the activities of Bill Sikes, Charley Bates, and other fictional characters, but he or she also "copies" that description into the extradiegetic world in which she or he lives. Dickens and his readers fully appreciate how the description of Jacob's Island could expand indefinitely in the atmosphere of the characters' frenetic and even desperate actions. Both understand the power that this generates by not allowing it to do so. Unstable description is harnessed to narrative drive and thereby increases its own intensity. Fiction outstrips without overstepping reality, and Jacob's Island takes its place in Western culture's encyclopedia. Dickens's social purpose, his open ideological endeavor, seeks to influence its audience in a way that Hardy's and Brontë's do not. His description is a different rhetorical gesture arising out of a different intentionality.

It appears that we have much work to do in the largely overlooked domain of description. Descriptions in fictional texts clearly include a broad range of functions and may constitute privileged sites for interpretation. Description also seems to recall into critical service tools such as intentionality, which have in recent years been seriously devalued. Dickens's description of Jacob's Island, appearing where it does in the narrative of *Oliver Twist,* accomplishes a special purpose, as I have tried to indicate.

What I am arguing is that not only is there a truth value in literature that can affect the "real" world, but that that value may be more potent in its way than the same value in a nonfictional work. A work of art might not change the real world in the way the Declaration of Independence did, but it could inspire men to seek the aims stated in that document. Dickens might have been writing just a novel, but his intention was clearly to do more than merely amuse and entertain. If he had no political objective, he certainly had a moral one. *Oliver Twist* is a made-up story, but the power of its fable and the vividness of its characters lend force to the real world in which its events are supposed to take place. It is notable that Jacob's Island did not exist in Sir Peter Laurie's hard-headed, "real" London, though he was an alderman of that city and presumably something of an expert about it. But Jacob's Island became real to a very large audience once it was represented in the fictional work of Charles Dickens. Ever after it was emphatically what it had been obscurely before—a real part of London. By including a description of a real place in a fictional text and exploiting readerly expectations of how both description and narration can work, Dickens was able to make his readers experience more acutely the real world of which they were a part, and it is testimony to the power of fiction that readers today can do so as well.

Although I have focused on a very small part of *Oliver Twist,* I have done so mainly to show that Dickens was a special kind of writer. While employing many realist techniques, such as elaborate description, or extensive metonymy (see chapter 4), he utilized these techniques to a different purpose, just as he did with devices from other genres such as fable (later I discuss Dickens's use of personification, for example). Dickens's agenda is different from that of realism because he wanted his art to show, not necessarily on a first reading; he wanted his readers to enjoy and participate in his texts as though they were equal partners, only in the end to reveal his control and the working out of his intentions as the author of the narrative. It is this feature of his work, I believe, that permitted him to accept description of himself as The Inimitable.

CHAPTER 2

Present Tense[1]

resent-tense narration is not very compatible with the general aims of realism. It shares some traits with first-person narration that make it undesirable. To begin with, it is more likely to introduce an unreliable narrator. A first-person narrator, even if recording past events, nonetheless introduces the subjectivity of an individual character. A powerful nineteenth-century example is Thackeray's *Barry Lyndon*. Thackeray signals Lyndon's unreliability by revealing that he is writing from prison, a hint at Lyndon's morally objectionable character. Present-tense narration could have the same "flaw" unless it is the historical present not identified with a specific narrator, but, in fiction, that is not usually the case. Realism generally aims at the provability of the chronicle, and therefore past-tense and third-person narration serve it best. First-person narration serves certain formulaic genres well, as in the traditional model of the adventure story such as Scott's *Rob Roy* or Stevenson's *Treasure Island* and *Kidnapped*. Modern detective fiction, from Conan Doyle to Raymond Chandler, gravitates toward first-person narration and sometimes present-tense narration. But present-tense narration has an added quality that sets it aside from most other forms of narration—its radical uncertainty. If one is actually writing/narrating at the moment that events are taking place, no outcome can be predicted safely. It is largely this quality that makes present-tense narration unattractive to realist fiction, which often seeks to establish predictable lines of development, whether through social situations, heredity, character formation, or any other broad influence. Some modern novelists have been able to combine first-person narration with a deep concern about the human condition. I think first of Albert Camus. But then, because of their philosophical content and fabular construction, I would definitely not put Camus' fiction in the genre of realism. Collins and Dickens experimented with present-tense narration while trying to preserve authorial control and while adhering to a providential view of human existence. This was not an easy purpose to achieve, but I believe both succeeded in their different ways.

The present tense in fiction was not new when Charles Dickens and Wilkie Collins came to make use of it. *Clarissa* and other diary and epistolary novels had exploited the mode long before. Such novels gained the advantage, through present tense, of making the events of their narratives appear immediate.[2] Moreover, by restricting the narrative voice or voices to the present, there could be little chance for a premature revelation of what was to occur in the future of the narrative. Aside from these modes of present tense, the traditional novel did make use of present tense in third-person narratives. As Christine Brooke-Rose points out, however, "in nineteenth-century fiction, brief passages in the historic present are used for vivid scenes before safe returns to the past, and the present tense is favoured for universalizing moral or social comments from the author" (12).[3] Dickens and Collins in their use of the present tense anticipate experiments with tense in the twentieth century, including Modernist and *nouveau roman* fiction. But whereas twentieth-century narratives exploiting present tense are chiefly concerned to liberate the narrative from the tyranny of the narrator, as in the fiction of Alain Robbe-Grillet, Dickens and Collins used the device to strengthen the narrative voice's power by taking command of the future and withholding its secrets from the reader.

In what follows, I shall examine how Collins and especially Dickens use present-tense narration in a way that violates recent thinking about "historical" narration and how, in doing so, they increase authorial control. Collins employs the traditional device of a present-tense text embedded in an otherwise past-tense narrative, but Dickens is more innovative. In fact, Christian Paul Casparis, one of a few critics to deal extensively with present-tense narration, credits Dickens with being the first novelist "to use the Present tense in a structured manner on a large scale" (62). My discussion of Collins's and Dickens's use of present tense will require brief preliminary discussions of the role of tense in narration and of the providential esthetic of nineteenth-century literature.

· · ·

In *Problems in General Linguistics,* Emile Benveniste drew a helpful distinction between two planes of utterance, that of history and that of discourse. *History* is delimited, in terms of tense, to three possibilities—the aorist (simple past), the imperfect, and the pluperfect. It excludes everything "autobiographical," especially the present tense (206–7). By contrast, *discourse* is free to use all tenses except the aorist (209). Benveniste defines present tense as "'the time at which one is speaking.' This is the eternally 'present' moment, although it never relates to the same events of an 'objective' chronology because it is determined for each speaker by each of the instances of discourse related to it. Linguistic time is *self-referential.* Ultimately, human temporality with all its linguistic apparatus reveals the subjectivity inherent in the very using of language" (227). In associating discourse with subjectivity and language with the possibility of subjectivity, Benveniste seems to reinforce the separation of history, the narration of past events, and discourse, the more broadly conceived plane of language use. I shall argue, however, that it is precisely across the boundaries of history and discourse that Collins and Dickens achieve some remarkable effects, effects that, in our own day might be most closely identified with cinema.

Aside from writers like Christian Paul Casparis, few narratologists have paid much attention to present-tense narration. Seymour Chatman remarks that "verbal narratives in English are occasionally written in the present tense. But story-time is still usually the past" (83). He also observes that cinema is the medium most clearly associated with real-time narration (84). Shlomith Rimmon-Kenan cites one type of narration that "is simultaneous with the action, e.g. reporting or diary entries," and gives Butor's *La Modification* as an example. Rimmon-Kenan does not pursue this narrative possibility. Most narratologists seem to take for granted the position that Philip J. M. Sturgess, following Gerald Prince's treatment of the subject in *Narratology,* summarizes thus:

> To narrate is also to commit oneself to a tense of narration, with that of the past tense being overwhelmingly the elected mode. Unlike the present tense which has, so to speak, contingency and even the possibility of sudden closure or cancellation built into it, the past tense seems to offer a guarantee of narrativity since it denotes a certainty of temporal duration, extending to whatever (present) temporal vantage point the narrator may be understood

to be narrating from. Within such duration, obviously enough, events and situations can be understood to have occurred, people to have lived and perhaps died. In other words the past tense is narrativizable in a way that the present tense does not suggest itself to be. (23)

But it is precisely the possibility of "sudden closure or cancellation," among other uncertainties, that makes present tense an attractive method for creating anxieties and exploiting uncertainty. Dorrit Cohn, picking up Gérard Genette's expression "simultaneous narrating," goes on to demonstrate how present-tense narration can avoid two prominent conventions of fictional realism, first-person fictional narration and the interior monologue, by "dissolving the semantic specificity that attends the historical present," thus encouraging the reader "to understand the present as a temporally indeterminate or 'absolute' narrative tense, for which the most appropriate term—highlighting its fiction-specificity—would seem to be 'fictional present'" (106). She explains that whereas the fictional diary or letter may shrink the temporal hiatus to hours or even minutes, simultaneous narration reduces it to zero, "the moment of narration is the moment of experience, the narrating self is the experiencing self" (107). As we shall see, this is the distinction between Collins's and Dickens's use of present-tense narration, the full impact of which does not seem to have registered with their critics.[4] Part of their narrative strategy was determined by what has been called the providential esthetic, which establishes a difference between their use of present-tense narration and its use by such modern authors as John Fowles, J. M. Coetzee, Margaret Atwood, and others.

There now exists a tradition of critical writing that accepts the significance of providence as a narrative ally in literature of the eighteenth and nineteenth century in England.[5] Generally this critical view admits that an assumption of providential design lies behind many of the ultimately positive narrative schemes produced by British novelists. Often the providential design was openly acknowledged. But developments during the nineteenth century, including the theory of evolution propounded by Charles Darwin and others, problematized the notion of providential control and introduced an anxiety about the future that was new in kind. Sir Arthur Conan Doyle remembered the mood of that midcentury time:

[F]rom my reading and from my studies, I found that the foundations not only of Roman Catholicism but of the whole Christian faith, as presented to me in nineteenth century theology, were so weak that my mind could not build upon them. It is to be remembered that these were the years when Huxley, Tyndall, Darwin, Herbert Spencer and John Stuart Mill were our chief philosophers, and that even the man in the street felt the strong sweeping current of their thought, while to the young student, eager and impressionable, it was overwhelming. (26)

In general, both Dickens and Collins employed the providential pattern to one degree or another in their novels, but the openness of the future also became for them an intriguing counterpoint to the directedness of providential designs. Because present tense is blind to the future, it was an excellent tool for exploiting anxiety about the outcomes of narratives.

. . .

Wilkie Collins's utilization of present-tense narration to manipulate his audience is relatively conventional. It is his insertion of Marian Halcombe's narrative in *The Woman in White* (1860) that is most relevant to my exploration of the inventive ways in which Victorian writers play with narrative structure in order to exploit their readers' fears about the future. Marian's voice is remarkably strong; the reader can hardly help but like her, and, in fact, some have even fallen in love with her.[6] However, rather than listening for *what* we hear in her voice, it will be more profitable for us to look at *how* we hear Marian's story. It is in this facet of the narration that we see both Collins's achievement with regard to narrative form and his genius for generating suspense. Peter Thoms points out that early detective fiction "not only reflects authorial exuberance in intricate plotting but also reveals an extensive critique of narrative patterns and the compulsions that generate them" (3). Collins's manipulation of the narrative was quite purposeful, and it can be no accident that the revelation of Marian's story takes place under the very controlled circumstances that I shall now detail.

Before dealing specifically with Marian's testimony, it is worthwhile to provide a brief review of the structure of Collins's novel as a whole. *The Woman in White*, like *The Moonstone* (1868), consists of a series of first-person narratives compiled by one character in order to guide the reader through the unraveling of a mystery. It is constructed as if we are reading individual testimony, and much has been written on the ways in which Collins's experimentation with this form resulted in a greater sense of mystery. Each eyewitness is allowed to reveal only his or her own firsthand experiences, thus effectively eliminating any problems Collins might have had with a third-person narrator who, if omniscient, would have had sometimes to withhold information in order to maintain suspense and mystery. But the analysis we are working toward has to move beyond discussing simply that brilliant aspect of Collins's novels. It is important to note that while we hear the voices of individual characters, they do not truly speak for themselves; they are, in effect, edited.[7] Individual testimonial texts, such as transcribed accounts, series of letters, diaries, and so forth, reach the reader only after they have passed under the pen of the editing character. In *The Woman in White,* this character is Walter Hartright, and it is only through him that we hear the voices of the other characters. Sometimes their stories, as in the case of Mrs. Catherick, are culled from letters that are addressed to Hartright himself. Most of the time the accounts are written as documents, as in the cases of Vincent Gilmore and Eliza Michelson. But these are still directed to Hartright, as is demonstrated by Gilmore who begins, "I write these lines at the request of my friend, Mr. Walter Hartright" (127). These submitted testimonies offer us interesting venues for investigating various aspects of narration, but here we are concerned with one specific aspect best explored in the portion of the text described as "The Story continued by MARIAN HALCOMBE, in Extracts from her Diary" (163).

Diary writing enters into a mixed temporality: it is neither fully present, nor fully past. The diary entry generally records the immediate past, often-times what has transpired over the course of that same day.[8] As it describes an incident, the tense tends toward the past—*we breakfasted.*[9] But diaries are also immersed in their own present: the author *is* writing. As entries depict the setting in which they are being created, they may allude to that very instantaneous temporality—*I am sitting in the window seat in the parlor as I write this down*—and then return to reflections upon the past, which are easier to sustain. The diarist may also venture into the time of the future, but it is generally only possible for the writer to do so in the most uncertain of terms—*tomorrow we depart: will I ever look upon these walks and gardens again?* In her work on both the diary (nonfictive) and the diary novel, Lorna Martens determines that the diarist "cannot foresee what will happen or what he will think on any future date, and if he keeps his diary as a general record, he cannot predict what he will write about in the future. The diary is thus a form that eludes the author's full control" (33). Therefore, as the diarist records his or her present, there can be no true foreshadowing of what is to come: the writer has absolutely no idea of the way in which things will work themselves out or even which incidents are important. The same is not true for the novelist who employs a diarist in her fiction. She may still fit the diary into the overall narrative design.

Herein lies the brilliance of Collins allowing Marian to speak only in this medium. In a diary, all kernels of information are equal in that they have yet to be judged with an eye to the end. Even though a reader of the novel might be fully aware of the author's (Collins's) control of the diarist's entries, he/she cannot know what the author intends to reveal anymore than he/she can surmise what is unknown as yet to the diarist. The diarist might place greater emphasis on some happenings or observations than on others, but then readers must determine whether or not they trust the character's intuitiveness (a term which I am here differentiating from reliability) before they can decide if the diary's hierarchy of information is accurate. So, as the Victorian reader entered into the narrative of the diary, he or she would have been, as we still are, forced to question Marian's ability to record clues to the future. Marian herself questions this ability. In her self-examination of advice she has given to Hartright, she writes, "Except Laura, I never was more anxious about anyone than I am now about Walter. All that has happened since he left us has only increased my strong regard for him. I hope I am doing right in trying to help him to employment abroad—I hope, most earnestly and anxiously that it will end well" (177).[10] Here, independent of an editorial time, Marian has access only to the near past and her immediate present as she attempts to analyze her situation and predict the outcome of her actions. Her diary provides a perfect medium through which the Victorian reader can be confronted with questions of knowledge and destiny. By examining what is important today, is it possible to find traces of what will be imperative in the future? Does Fate foreshadow? Does Providence guide?

Of course, Collins complicates this inquiry into the future by sometimes suggesting that this particular Victorian quest is an anxious occupation in its own right. Anticipating the marriage of Laura to Sir Glyde, Marian herself is conflicted by her construction of the tomorrows that stretch endlessly before her. "I am writing of the marriage and the parting with Laura, as people write of a settled thing. It seems so old and so unfeeling to be looking at the future already in this cruelly composed way" (187). The pursuit of knowledge will continue as the marriage preparations unfold; and, again, the reader is put in a position parallel to that of the character speaking. Because Marian is recording her impressions as they occur to her, we are given mistaken and contradicting accounts of Glyde. "19th.—More discoveries in the inexhaustible mine of Sir Percival's virtues" (192); "20th.—I hate Sir Percival!" (194). However, this ambivalence does not erode Marian's credibility; it simply intensifies the reader's sense of sharing the present-tense temporality of the speaker. After Sir and Lady Glyde return to England and establish themselves and their guests at Blackwater Park, Laura confides her anxieties to Marian: "Every fresh thing he does, seems to terrify me about the future" (253). If central characters fear the future, what must the reader feel? Through the temporal form of the diary, one lacking the consistency and confidence of hindsight, readers are able to experience the same apprehensions and uncertainties as Marian and Laura. There is no frame that can establish a retrospective analysis of events, so when Marian writes, "I almost dread tomorrow," so too can the reader! (259).

Martens tells us that "the diary novel . . . emphasizes the time of writing rather than the time that is written about" (4). Thus, while Marian's diary provides us with clues to what deviousness Fosco and Glyde are concocting, the emphasis is on Marian's vulnerability. The very introduction of her diary into the narrative heightens its suspense since the reader cannot be sure that Marian herself has survived from the time of her documenting into the time of the compiling. Todorov tells us that "the movement [in suspense] is from cause to effect: we are first shown the causes . . . and our interest is sustained by the expectation of what will happen" (47). Collins's suspense is not that of gangsters (cause) and corpses (effect), but of diary (the medium through which Marian speaks) and absent writer (why else would a woman hand over the record of her most private thoughts?). It is this twist that demonstrates Collins's ingenious understanding of what might frighten his audience—he played on their fears of not having the means to know the end. Marian's section of the narrative ends with the same insinuation of absence—"NOTE. At this place the entry in the diary ceases to be legible. . . . On the next page of the Diary, another entry appears. It is in a man's handwriting . . ." (343). The astute reader, by now fully able to recognize his diction, need not wait for Count Fosco's signature. His intruding comments offer a sinister picture of the now occluded future. "I breathe my wishes for her recovery. I condole with her on the inevitable failure of every plan that she has formed for her sister's benefit . . . Fosco" (344).

On January 28, 1860, readers would have received the tenth installment of the serialization which opens with Marian's diary. Tension would have begun to build at that point in time. However, it can be said that because of the ongoing sense of the entries, the crisis does not make itself overt until Fosco's violation of the diary. This would have occurred in the 22nd installment of the serialization which was published on April 21, 1860. The revelation that Marian never left Blackwater ends the 25th installment on May 12, 1860. For almost five months, but most especially during this aforementioned three-week period, the reader would have been left in doubt as to whether Marian spoke through her diary by choice or by necessity—that is, whether she was still available to speak at all. As the 25th installment ends, Marian is presumably alive, although the Victorian reader would still have had to endure a painful anticipation before another installment verified this. In effect, the reader would have lived through a very convincing simulacrum of what the characters in the book were living through.

In general, the narrative constitutes a *history* in which the compilation of information by Hartright causes most of the "documents" to be a past-tense discussion of events from a time—the time of their creation *for* Hartright—which is actually forward of the time in which the mystery would have reached its climax. Thus the reader is assured that the story as a whole is one read through a retrospective filter which was constructed only after some conclusion (albeit one unknown to the reader) had been reached. Collins knew that his Victorian readers more than anything desired a sense of closure. They were searching for the meaning this would provide for their own lives—a reinforcement of the concepts of both providence and destiny. However, as Lonoff points out to us, Collins also wanted to write a suspenseful novel that would be more popular and profitable for its manipulation of his readers' anxieties. He does this most effectively through the *discourse* of Marian's diary by forcing the reader into a simulation of what it would have been like to live out the events in the story in the present tense of their happening, thereby exploiting their fears that some other force, such as chance or malign human intent, might prevail if not in the narrative as a whole, then in the fate of one of its most appealing characters.[11] However, as Cohn points out, no matter how immediate the temporal sensation of a diary might be, it cannot achieve the zero temporality she associates with simultaneous narration. The reader always knows that the diary is a document completed up to a certain point before the reader reads it. Despite Collins's skill in exploiting present-tense narration in order to enhance suspense and strengthen his narrative authority, his approach is nonetheless conventional. The same is not true of Dickens.

Dickens makes extended use of present-tense narration in three of his mature novels—*Bleak House, Our Mutual Friend,* and *The Mystery of Edwin Drood.*[12] In *Bleak House* the third-person narrative voice speaks in the present tense with a Jeremiah-like authority, which contrasts with Esther Summerson's humble and subjective first-person, past-tense narration. The third-person narrative voice's chapters are more panoramic than dramatic. They pass judgment and summarize actions. They address large issues concerning society. Now and then they become intensely dramatic, but often still remain without dialogue. The best example is the presentation of the events leading up to and following Krook's extinction by spontaneous combustion. In *Our Mutual Friend* there is no obvious division of narrative voices. The whole text is narrated in the third person. But now and then a chapter is narrated in the present tense. These present-tense chapters generally are concerned with public or quasi-public events, such as the activities of Veneering and his associates surrounding his decision to run for Parliament. These chapters consist almost entirely of panoramic presentation. But Dickens's use of the present tense in *The Mystery of Edwin Drood* is an advance in technique upon these two employments of the tense.

Like Collins, Dickens played upon his readers' anxieties about an uncertain future, while nonetheless endorsing a providential certainty about the nature of human existence, and in doing so both thrilled and entertained them. In *Bleak House* the subjective narrative of Esther Summerson is narrated in traditional past tense of *history*, but surprisingly the third-person narrator records events in the present tense in a way that recalls Carlyle's experiments in historical writing.[13] The third-person narrator approximates the mode of cinema, where the camera, with all of its real-time immediacy, can show us surfaces in great detail, but makes few attempts to penetrate them. *Bleak House* forces *history* and *discourse* to inhabit a single text, leaving the reader to puzzle out the significance of the suspense and satisfaction created by this abutment. Ironically, it is Esther's "autobiographical" narrative that employs the presumably nonautobiographical and nonsubjective past-tense mode of history, and the objective, historically oriented third-person narrator who employs the subjective mode of discourse. *Our Mutual Friend* complicates this conjunction of planes of utterance by removing the "simplification" of having two distinct narrators. Now the same narrative voice shifts from the manner of history to that of discourse, from past-tense omniscience to present-tense cinematic exploration of surfaces. But in *The Mystery of Edwin Drood,* the device is taken to a new level because now one narrative voice slides between history and discourse, but the present-tense chapters permit a transcending of surfaces, so that internal conditions can be revealed, as in cinema voice-over, symbolism, fade-ins to mental states, and so forth can reveal unexpressed states of mental action, such as dreams and desires.[14] Dickens has finally established his past-tense narrative as history and his present-tense narrative as discourse, according to Benveniste's distinction, but he has done so in a single narrative in which the two modes continually, but covertly, manifest their mutual incompatibility.[15]

Another problem that surfaces when contrasting the use of present-tense narration in *Bleak House* and *The Mystery of Edwin Drood* is that of focalization, the means by which the events of a narrative are perceived. There is still no certain agreement about how to define focalization, but for my purposes here I shall define it as the mediating vantage point from which events in the narrative are seen. Mieke Bal offers one of the broader explanations. "When focalization lies with one character which participates in the fabula as an actor, we could refer to *internal* focalization. We can then indicate by means of the term external focalization that an anonymous agent, situated outside the fabula is functioning as focalizer" (105).[16] Many narratologists, following Gérard Genette, argue that the focalizer must be a figure in the fabula, not a nondiegetic voice.[17]

In *Bleak House* there are essentially no focalizing characters in the present-tense narration, but the ideological position of the narrating voice located outside the fabula is so apparent that that voice occasionally cannot help but blurt out his position, as in this notorious example just after Jo the crossing sweeper has died.

> The light is come upon the dark benighted way. Dead!
> Dead, your Majesty. Dead, my lords and gentlemen. Dead, Right Reverends and Wrong Reverends of every order. Dead, men and women, born with Heavenly compassion in your hearts. And dying thus around us every day. (649)[18]

Something more complicated is happening in *The Mystery of Edwin Drood*. Like *Bleak House*, *Drood* begins in the present tense. The first character introduced is John Jasper in an opium den. "Shaking from head to foot, the man whose scattered consciousness has thus fantastically pieced itself together, at length rises, supports his trembling frame upon his arms, and looks around. He is in the meanest and closest of small rooms" (1). But where is the narrator? Not only is he in the present tense, but he is also either in Jasper's head or else on some other spatial and temporal plane—the passage opens with a description of a cathedral and dissolves into fragmented references to a Sultan, Turkish robbers, and a royal procession complete with ten thousand scimitars and white elephants! The narrator and the narrative sustain this strange construction of temporality until the sixth and seventh chapters, when the narrative shifts temporarily to past tense.[19] This first present-tense narration's focalization is blurred from the outset. The narrator is capable of knowing what the dreaming John Jasper sees. Are we to understand that Jasper is the focalizer here even as he dreams? I think not. His vision is mediated through the narrator and I am prepared to call that focalization. But the focalization does not rest there. When Jasper comes to consciousness it shifts to him as he looks on with disgust at Princess Puffer and a drugged lascar. Moreover, in the last pages of the novel, focalization hovers between the narrator and Datchery. Dickens, in this novel, seems to be treating focalization as a version of free indirect discourse, where boundaries of definition can also blur and dissolve quickly. The present-tense narrator of *Bleak House* was a remote surveyor of surfaces. By contrast the narrative voice of *Drood* is so intimate and invasive that it can describe the images in dreams and can know what the characters think. In fact, in some of these instances it appears as though the simultaneous narration is compromised and that the narrator is providing an account of events that have already transpired, most notably in the chapter that describes events the night before Drood's disappearance. Here is an example:

Edwin Drood passes a solitary day. Something of deeper moment than he had thought has gone out of his life, and in the silence of his own chamber he wept for it last night. Though the image of Miss Landless still hovers in the background of his mind, the pretty little affectionate creature, so much firmer and wiser than he had supposed, occupies its stronghold. (124)

A similar passage describes Jasper's day.

John Jasper passes a more agreeable and cheerful day than either of his guests. Having no music-lessons to give in the holiday season, his time is his own, but for the Cathedral services. He is early among the shopkeepers, ordering little table luxuries that his nephew likes. His nephew will not be with him long, he tells his provision-dealers, and so must be petted and made much of. (127–28)

I would argue that this is not historical present—the present-tense narration of events already past—but a compacted version of simultaneous narration. It resembles the technique Dickens used in *David Copperfield* where David provides condensed accounts of his early history in present-tense chapters he calls retrospects. These are historical present accounts. But the condensed descriptions of Drood's and Jasper's days are condensed within the present-tense narration of ongoing experience, a characteristic emphasized by the parallel presentation ("Edwin Drood passes ..." "John Jasper passes ...").

I am suggesting that Dickens was making some remarkable advances in narrative craft and that an examination of his use of present-tense narration is one avenue through which to disclose them. However, whereas modern novelists have carried such experiments a long way for new purposes, Dickens remained committed to authorial control. He did this to a great extent in *Drood* by dwelling upon what is not known.

While a number of Dickens's novels deal with mystery as a crime that must be solved or as the unknowable destiny that awaits each character, only one of his works—as its title suggests—specifically sets out to be a suspense novel: *The Mystery of Edwin Drood*. Like his earlier work, this book also poses questions of how much control characters have over their own lives. Rosa Bud and Edwin Drood, for example, feel themselves trapped in an arranged betrothal that has determined the course of their futures in a way that they themselves might not have arranged those tomorrows. And John Jasper feels himself trapped in what to him is the trivial existence of a cathedral choir director. Present-tense narration, more specifically simultaneous narration, enhances this sense of entrapment at the same time that it increases immediacy. It emphasizes contingency. But this is a psychological contingency, not the material contingency of realism. It is as though Dickens is consciously substituting the one for the other to emphasize the fabular/ imaginative quality over any resemblance it has to realism.

The absence of a frame complicates and enriches *Drood*. As with the third-person narrators of *Bleak House* and *Our Mutual Friend*, there is no suggestion that the narrator exists within the story itself, despite his present-tense discourse.[20] There is also no reference that would allow us to read *Drood* as a memoir, for example, a text that can plausibly use the present tense to re-create past incidents. Instead, the reader is caught up in the moment as it actually occurs and experiences the events in the same temporality as do the characters. Of course, the reader cannot actually ever get past the fact that he or she is situated elsewhere, in the study or on the couch *reading* the story instead of living the events. But it is a compliment to Dickens's talent that the reader's reality rarely interferes with the development of the story and that no ruptures occur in the narrative which would jolt the reader back to the fact that it is highly implausible that someone would have been able to follow along with *all* of the events *as* they actually happened. Indeed, the shifts back to past tense emphasize the unusualness of the present-tense chapters. Dickens is calling attention to their transgressive nature. Working ostensibly toward a "mystery" narrative, Dickens has created an even deeper level of suspense in his creation of a third-person narrator who is able to pass judgment on characters and their actions, but who is never put into the position of seeming to withhold information from the reader. There is nothing in Dickens's text from which the reader can infer that the narrator holds the secret of the mystery; the reader simply accepts that he or she will follow the present-tense description of events until the conclusion (or, as should have been the case, the solution). Strikingly, the present-tense narration, with its blindness of the future, dominates the past-tense narration, which, because it is in the past tense and hence presumably subsequent to events it describes, should overwhelm the present-tense narration through its supposed access to the outcome of events. That it does not is apparent in the opaqueness of *Drood*'s plot. No one has been able satisfactorily to finish Dickens's story. Dickens, an already astute judge of his audience's desire for social justice and personal security, has tapped into what would have been one of his readers' greatest fears: that life is a mystery enshrouding each individual and that no single clue exists which can lift that mantle and reveal the future.

Although the present-tense sections of *Drood* play upon the reader's anxiety by withholding any information about what is to come, they can nonetheless create an atmosphere of mystery and even dread. A relatively innocuous example occurs when John Jasper looks in upon his sleeping nephew, Edwin Drood. "His nephew lies asleep, calm and untroubled. John Jasper stands looking down upon him, his unlighted pipe in his hand, for some time, with a fixed and deep attention. Then, hushing his footsteps, he passes to his own room, lights his pipe, and delivers himself to the Spectres it invokes at midnight" (38). The apprehension experienced in reading this passage comes not only from previous knowledge of Jasper, but, even more deliberately, from the sense that nobody, not even the narrator, truly knows what is lurking and lying in wait and, thus, everyone who ventures into that next moment known as the future is vulnerable. By intimating that signs do exist, sometimes in the form of heavy thunderclouds and other times in the cast of a sunny day, Dickens is toying with his readers' desperate desire to read their own personal and cultural climate. Perhaps Dickens is directly addressing this desire when he describes, in a third-person section of the novel, Mr. Grewgious's meditation upon the heavens.

> [H]is gaze wandered from the windows to the stars, as if he would have read in them something that was hidden from him. Many of us would, if we could; but none of us so much as know our letters in the stars yet—or seem likely to do it, in this state of existence—and few languages can be read until their alphabets are mastered. (160)

Expounding upon the concepts of destiny and providence is one of the ways in which Dickens is able to create the sense that there is "something-about-to-happen" without having to allude directly to the event itself. Were Dickens to do this, were he to allow his present-tense narrator to know things before they happen, Dickens would be breaking the narrator's temporal boundaries. One of the few theorists to deal with the present tense in narration is Gary Saul Morson. He writes of the professional requirements of a sportscaster that "in the temporality of his narration, there cannot be foreshadowing. On the contrary everything in his voice is oriented toward the present and the *unknown* future" (177, emphasis added). Christian Paul Casparis calls such activities as sports announcing "current report" and relates this category of present-tense usage to what he calls the historical present by its inability to know the causal framework of the event in progress; the historical present narrative similarly manifests "a conscious or unconscious indifference to the causal linking of events" (151).

Past-tense narration can be mute about the future. It can forego prolepsis and limit itself to the events as they transpire, moving as close to sheer story (the chronological order of events) as possible, and avoiding the maneuvers of plot (the rearrangements of and refinements upon story). It can, in short, approach the condition of historical-present narration. It is even possible for present-tense narration to make use of prolepsis. That the narration is in the present tense does not mean that the future is not fully known to the narrator. An example of this possibility within Dickens's own work is *David Copperfield,* where the present-tense retrospective chapters occur within David's autobiography of which he has complete knowledge. What is to prevent the narrator from writing something like this? "David sits at the window, watching travelers pass in the street. The day will come when he too will be one of those travelers. But now his wondering gaze rests upon a parade of strangers." This is present-tense narration resembling historical-present narration. Such a liberty would presumably violate the conventions of simultaneous narration, the method, I am arguing, of *Drood.*

What is striking about *The Mystery of Edwin Drood* is that both present- and past-tense chapters withhold knowledge of the future. It is the muteness about the future in the past-tense chapters that enhances a similar muteness in the present-tense chapters. The inability or refusal of Dickens's narrator to claim an already complete knowledge of the story would have disturbed a nineteenth-century reader more perhaps than grisly hints of horrors to come. The opaqueness of the future, rather than specific references to forth-coming adventures, would have unnerved the reader. It is the opposite effect to that created by the use of prolepsis, when a narrator anticipates an event to come, especially an unpleasant or even fatal event, as when a narrator says, "If only he had known at that moment what was to occur the very next day." This disclosure of a future event can create suspense and anxiety in a reader, but it is a different order of suspense from the blank future of present-tense simultaneous narration.

One of the ways in which Morson differentiates between "sports time" and a novel is his claim that a reader can always close a book, read its last page, or perhaps read an introduction that explains the plot. He writes, "the outcome has in a sense already happened . . . rather than [being] of real contingency in our own present" (174).[21] Thus, no matter how mysterious or threatening the circumstances might appear, there is always the underlying suggestion that it is all already over, already done, and that nothing in the reading of the narrative can happen to change the ending of the story. Most readers have probably sensed an impending resolution, even when narrative events appear at their most tangled, simply because there is a diminishing number of pages separating them from where they are in the story and the last page of the book. When it becomes obvious that there is only one chapter or one page left, even the least savvy of readers can see that the finale draws closer and that the circumstances of the story must be resolved. Thus, by the sheer passing of turned pages, an adventure that began with an infinite number of possibilities must at last come down to only one—the end. However, because both Collins and Dickens first published their work in serial form, it is arguable that for their audiences there would have been a greater sense of an open ending. Since it would have been easily recognized that both authors alluded to current events, readers would have been aware that the stories were being written *even as they read*.[22] This would have undermined the reader's sense that the characters' futures were foretold—that the events were long over—and would have intensified the readers' anxiety as to what the next installment of the characters' lives might mean for them. Through the medium of serial publication, which would have reinforced the effects of the present-tense narration, a feeling of contingency would have been more firmly established in the text. Again, this would have mimicked the same tension that confronted readers in their anxieties over their personal lives and the future generally. Who could know what tomorrow might bring?

It is with regard to the very human desire to know the ends of our own stories that Kermode gives new meaning to the concept of literacy. "The world is our beloved codex . . . we do, living as reading, like to think of it as a place where we can travel back and forth at will, divining congruences, conjunctions, opposites; extracting secrets from its secrecy . . . this is the way we satisfy ourselves with explanations of the unfollowable world—as if it were a structured narrative" (145). Victorian readers would have found that any alterations in the conventions of the novel, such as the insertion of a present-tense narration that disallows a foretold future, would have been simply one more way in which the author could force them to acknowledge their inability to read or write the future. Collins and Dickens, in their different ways, made sure that readers could not read their texts in the old familiar way—with the comfort of past-tense temporality and the reassurances of an omniscient narrator. Instead, both authors insisted that their readers confront the characters' situations as if they were themselves living in, if not the same circumstance, at least the same temporality. And by interrupting the traditional *history* narrative with the real-time impression of *discourse*, they allowed for a further examination of the questions of providence and destiny—not simply as narrative constructions, but as actual forces in the working out of events. By withholding any hints of the future in their present-tense narrations, thereby increasing their audiences' anxieties about it, they strengthened their own command over it, thus conferring on themselves the power of providential or fateful control that the present-tense itself seemed to deny. Just as promises of religion and philosophy could only be hoped for, not known for certain, so the reader of these present-tense narratives received no proleptic promises of a comfortable conclusion. But, like the scientists examining the physical relics of the past to construct a narrative of human existence, they had to wait until the story was told before they could judge if it was providence, destiny, or chance that brought them to where they now stood. Ironically, it was by this, the most obviously contrived element of the narrative, the rude coupling of the supposedly discrete planes of utterance of *history* and *discourse,* that Collins and Dickens were able to make their stories that much more *real* to their readers. And it is exactly this contrivance that sets the novel outside the category of realism. The reality dealt with here is not the replication of material conditions, but the sense of mental and emotional participation under the guidance of a master.

CHAPTER 3

Naming

ames are important in literature. Although in serious literature names tend to be nondirective until characters' natures are manifested through actions, in many cases a name itself defines a character's nature or hints at it. Realism must avoid the appearance of using symbolic, suggestive, or illustrative names, since this practice calls attention to authorial intention, which the realist novel seeks to mask. The realist novelist cannot indulge in such play with her audience. But especially in comic literature, we willingly accept names that typify. We accept them as a writer's shorthand, a way of conveying quickly and without complication the basic "humor" of his character. But we tend also to accept this shorthand passively, without considering the immense power that such naming confers upon the writer. In this chapter, I wish to explore the ways in which Dickens exploits a wide range of possibilities in the naming of characters as a means of sequestering the force of his narratives to his own authority, a gesture at odds with the conventions of realism which seek to create the illusion of transparent or "natural" narrative. Moreover, it is my contention that Dickens purposely uses names to call attention to his own performance, as the force behind naming both within and beyond the diegesis, thus purposely opposing the transparency supposed in realism.[1] Dickens's contemporaries were aware of his skill in naming and the interest has continued through Elizabeth Hope Gordon's *The Naming of Characters in the Works of Charles Dickens* (1917) to the present day.

The power of naming shows itself in many types of fiction, sometimes in quite subtle ways. At one point in Proust's *Remembrance of Things Past,* for example, Marcel refers to Rachel as "Rachel when from the Lord," a puzzling denomination for the general reader. J. Hillis Miller remarks that this is "a striking example within the novel itself of naming as a sovereign speech act making or remaking the one who is named" (*Speech Acts* 207). Miller emphasizes that, while Marcel's act of naming is part of the diegesis, it is actually Proust, not his character, who wishes to *convey* the multiple significances of the allusive name. If it were his character who wished to transmit this information, Proust would presumably have confirmed or explained Marcel's reason for employing this name. Instead, it remains a mystery to all but the initiate, though it is possible that Proust felt the allusion to Jacques Halévy's opera *La juive* (*The Jewess* [1835]) would be evident to his contemporaries.[2] Whatever the case, it is possible to make a distinction between the author's power to name and the significance of the act of naming within the diegesis, which, as Miller brilliantly demonstrates, requires an energetic intertextual exercise on the part of the reader.

Miller calls naming a "sovereign speech act," thereby himself indirectly alluding to the sovereignty granted to Adam and Eve over Eden, when God assigned them the privilege of naming the beings and objects of their world. Naming is widely understood to embody power in language. Few speech acts have more sustained effect, with the exception of such dramatic utterances as "Off with his head!" and the like. Women influenced by feminist activism from the middle of the twentieth century acknowledged the power of naming by refusing to yield the surname they were born with to take that of a husband, despite the fact that both names came to them from men. Stage names, pseudonyms, and aliases also indicate a strong human impulse to appropriate the power of naming to oneself. What concerns me in this chapter, beyond a general interest in Charles Dickens's practice of naming in his fiction, is the distinction hinted at, but not explored in depth in Miller's comments on Proust, between the author's and the narrator's or character's acts of naming.

Charles Dickens was acutely aware of the power of naming both within his narratives, as exercised by his characters or his narrators, and on his own part as author. From the beginning of his career, Dickens was deeply involved with and interested in the act of naming.[3] He began his writing career, as we all know, under a false name as Boz and relished such self-naming as The Inimitable, and the Sparkler of Albion. But from the *Sketches* onward, he was conscious of the resonances of names, most often in the early works for their comic qualities, a feature he shared with and borrowed from the numerous comic writers of his own and earlier times. Jingle aptly suggests the garrulousness of that character, as Winkle, Tupman, and less effectively Snodgrass suggest the respective characters of these humorous sidekicks. Pickwick itself is a comical name. Similarly, names that carry an allegorical quality were familiar in literary tradition and often used by some of Dickens's favorite writers. Henry Fielding's Squire Allworthy is a good example. Dickens's contemporary and friend Captain Frederick Marryat was in the habit of naming his protagonists according to their supposed or actual attributes, such as Peter Simple, Jacob Faithful, Masterman Ready, and Jack Easy.

Often the names Dickens selects have connotative value only, as with Quilp, a name that sounds both foolish and nasty. Other names suggest a character trait as with Miss Nipper and Mrs. MacStinger in *Dombey and Son*. Still others have associational power, as with Solomon Gills and Captain Cuttle, both connected to maritime activities. But some names also carry denotative power, as with Bradley Headstone, whose name was first tried in Dickens's notes as Amos Headstone or Deadstone, before becoming Bradley Deadstone and finally Headstone.[4] To thrust home his point, Dickens has Rogue Riderhood remark on the churchyard associations of the name. Michael Cotsell observes the resemblance of Fascination Fledgeby's name to "fledgling" (150). And, of course, there are the transparent Veneerings. There are even those well-known instances where Dickens borrowed directly or alluded satirically to real names, as he did with Fagin in *Oliver Twist*. All of these acts of naming by Dickens as author are significant. However, I am particularly interested in those instances where characters call attention to the act of naming, and, in doing so signal Dickens's own ultimate authority as the source of all such naming.

Garrett Stewart offers a good example of Dickens's complicated naming activity as early as *The Old Curiosity Shop*. Dick Swiveller achieves a kind of poetic apotheosis when he names the Brasses' anonymous servant girl the Marchioness. As Stewart puts it, he effectively brings the girl into being, a beingness that will be crucial to his recovery from illness and to his achieving a degree of success in life. But if Dick is something of a wordmaster and takes to himself the privilege of naming, he is himself, through Dickens's authority to name him, an example of the complex force that names can suggest. In Stewart's words:

Many have noted the importance of the name "Dick," one syllable of his author's last name, as a clue to the inherence in this comic character of at least a part of the author's own personality, one phase of his artistic temperament. Further, the family pronunciation of Sam's last name, "Veller," is also contained in Dick's own surname. And there is surely something in "Swiveller" that catches his directionless vitality, that willingness to take the prevailing wind which often makes him seem as though he is merely going in circles. But Dick not only swivels, he seeks; he himself wonders about his first name in connection with that prototypical Richard who became Lord Mayor of London. "Perhaps the bells might strike up 'Turn again, Swiveller, Lord Mayor of London.' Whittington's name was Dick." (105–6)

Stewart demonstrates the possible connections between Dickens and his character, the possible echoes between characters from different books, and the use of traditional lore to give weight to his own characters. The most significant attribute of this instance is its dual function: while it characterizes Dick, it also highlights the function of his name as a turner or swiveller. So, while Dick is focusing on his first name, Dickens is showing us the substance of his last name and hinting proleptically at Dick's ultimate turning from his trivial existence to a purposeful life.[5]

Stewart also points to some functions of naming in *Our Mutual Friend*. Again, it is characteristic for characters to manifest their own sense of superiority by naming others. So Eugene feels free to refer to Riah as "Mr. Aaron" and "Patriarch," claiming that he does so in a complimentary fashion, although, for the reader, his taking liberties with the Jew's name can be seen as a form of appropriation (Stewart 212). More telling is Stewart's example of self-naming in Jenny Wren. "Fanny Cleaver," he writes, "has bestowed upon herself a liberating pseudonym, a *nom de plumage* whose assonant lift is meant to carry her fancy above the sordidness of her cares and labors . . ." (205). Jenny sometimes smells flowers and hears songbirds that recall her dream of angelic visitors, and Stewart notes that "Jenny Wren has named herself a songbird—developing an eye as 'bright and watchful as the bird's whose name she had taken' (II,11)—and has grown herself a bower" (209). Jenny has consciously renamed herself with a view to redemption, or at least removal from her sordid reality. Stewart shrewdly remarks that, "Like Dickens himself, Jenny Wren is also a tireless coiner of names ironic and otherwise" for others (204). However, Stewart fails to note that it is Dickens who named this character Fanny Cleaver, whose ironic tongue is so sharp and cutting. Much as Jenny tries to wrest command of her character from her creator, he remains in control of her sardonic nature. His name for her—Cleaver—still fits. Moreover, it is also Dickens who has permitted Fanny to choose the name Jenny Wren, which has its ironies for her, but perhaps others for Dickens himself.[6]

David Copperfield offers a clear and simple example of the power of naming in an atmosphere of coercion within its diegesis.[7] When Mr. Murdstone wants to warn his associates to be prudent in their speech around the young David, he says someone is very sharp, identifying this someone as "Brooks of Sheffield," an allusion to the city of Sheffield's reputation for good cutlery.[8] Murdstone's humor here bears a surprising resemblance to some of Dickens's own metaphorical and metonymic naming techniques. Steerforth names David "Daisy," to indicate his innocence as well as his subjugation to Steerforth himself. In neither instance does David realize that the act of denomination is belittling and manipulative. Aunt Betsey renames David with her own name Trotwood as a mark of her command over him, just as Dora's nickname for him signifies possession. Harry Stone observes that the new name Trotwood also signals a new phase in David's life ("What's in a Name?" 193). The same could be said of Dora's nickname for David. David says that Doady is Dora's "corruption of David," an ambiguous statement. Dora is not a wise choice as a partner for a young man like David, and hence she does represent a "corruption" of his true course in life.[9] Within the narrative, therefore, it is clear that the act of naming involves an assumption of power over the person named (601). Oddly enough, David, who begins his career as an early story teller, seldom names other people in this way.

Personal names are intriguing in *David Copperfield* in various ways, one of which is the way they intimate rather than declare authorial intention. It is interesting how some of the important names in the novel suggest a natural setting—Copper*field*, Trot*wood*, Wick*field*, Murd*stone*. Arguably, these names suggest a pastoral quality in *Copperfield* that is more persistent than in most of Dickens's novels. In other novels, names of this sort also indicate characters who ultimately figure positively in their stories, such as *Wood*court and Light*wood*, whereas characters with names like Murd*stone* and Small*weed* suggest the unappealing aspects of the natural world. Even David's birthplace, Blunderstone, suggests the same outdoor atmosphere, though the "blunder" in the word implies error and misfortune and is therefore not pleasantly combined with the hard suggestions of "stone." The name is also a forecast of Clara Copperfield's second husband, the cruel Mr. Murdstone, whose name Betsey Trotwood confuses when she complains that David's mother "goes and marries a Murderer—or a man with a name like it . . ." (253). In passages such as this, Dickens calls attention to his own authority in the act of naming. Harry Stone indicates that Dickens's selection of the name Murdstone combines ideas of murder and hardness with equal emphasis and openness, but also shows how the name connects him with David's real father by way of its allusion to the father's gravestone ("What's in a Name?" 194–95). Some names including w's suggest weakness in character and include most notably Mr. Wilkins Micawber, but also Mr. Wickfield and both Dora Spenlow and her father, but others, especially those beginning with w's imply some degree of firmness, notably Weller and Westlock, but also Wardle and Wegg in their ways. Perhaps the most interesting is Wemmick, a character who seems to mirror the harsh traits of his employer, but who turns out, in his domestic character, to have a very soft side. But Dickens also tries out a pattern he uses effectively in *Great Expectations* by contrasting names with the same number of letters, though with different connotative sounds. Thus the steady and alert Mr. Peggotty is set against the glum and morose Mrs. Gummidge. More significant, perhaps, are the names of David's friendly companion and Steerforth's evil servant. Though Micawber's name may suggest weakness, its open vowels and soft consonants also imply a kindly, accommodating nature, whereas Littimer's pinched vowels and pointy consonants hint at a prickly, unappealing character.[10] Several characters' names are ambiguous. Hence, Steerforth itself calls up heroic possibilities, but, these possibilities are, as we discover by the end of the novel, misapplied. Tommy Traddles's name is both comic and balanced, and it is the combination of a humorous and an industrious character that brings him success in life.

What interests me in *Copperfield* is that it is Dickens, not his first-person narrator, who is in charge of this naming. The water imagery of this novel supports a complex pattern of danger, salvation, and death. Steerforth's name evokes the image of a sea captain, but this "hero" corrupts Little Em'ly and carries her off in his sailing vessel, a reversal of the ideal of the rescue at sea. And Steerforth dies retributively in both literal and metaphorical shipwreck. Dickens reinforces the moral design of his novel by showing the morally compassless Steerforth coming to misfortune through the abuse of his considerable powers.[11] By contrast, Peggotty keeps an ark that has come to rest not on Ararat, but the Yarmouth sands, where he shelters his extended family, including the appropriately named Ham, named after a son of the original ark owner, Noah. Ultimately, it is a ship that will carry the Micawbers, Em'ly, and Martha to a new world of opportunity in Australia. Dickens, not his characters, links appropriate names to a water-related theme by way of obliging his readers to interpret his narrative in the manner he directs, not in some capricious reading of their own. This aim on his part might be misguided, given the researches of modern critics, especially those employing what is known as reader-response criticism, but there is little doubt in my mind that this was his purpose.[12]

Dickens himself took delight in naming his characters, from the simplest and most theatrical to more subtle and complicated instances, but it is also interesting to observe the ways in which he delegates the authority for naming to his third-person and first-person narrators. Esther Summerson and David Copperfield tend not to be big namers, whereas third-person narrators name as freely as Dickens himself, if any distinction is to be made between author and narrator. The ironic voice of the narrator of *Our Mutual Friend* even dispenses with proper names, to call a few of the stylized characters Boots, Brewer, and, in a much slyer manner, the Veneering servant who is referred to as the Analytical Chemist.

Dickens was fully aware of what one might call the sins of naming. Michael Ragussis has shown the discordance between a person or place's name and its actual nature. In fact, he indicates that this discordance is part of a larger problem with language itself in *Bleak House,* arguing that "language is London's communicative/communicable disease" (263). Even Esther Summerson's apparently positive name is misleading; unlike other characters who are robbed of histories by their names, "it is not the name itself that robs her: it is the absence of a name" (257). But if Dickens offered numerous indications about the perils involved with naming, he also offered as many indications of his own authority and control where naming was concerned, and Ragussis, without making this case, gives an appropriate instance. Hawdon, Esther's unknown father, is referred to in several ways: the Captain, Nemo (his own alias), Our Dear Brother (the narrator's ironic term), and Nimrod, Mrs. Snagsby's misunderstanding of Nemo. But, as Ragussis demonstrates, this incorrect name referring to the mighty hunter of the Old Testament nonetheless connects Hawdon to the theme of confused language indicated by references to the tower of Babel and carried out in the thematic network of language as confusion in "Dickens's brilliant use of 'the great wilderness of London' (xlviii, 583), that 'immense desert of law-hand' (xlvii, 567), as the Old Testament desert, but with this difference: the Law of God, the divine Word, has itself degenerated into babel, and the Father has become the tyrannous, and dead, Pharaoh" (262). Thus, while confusion might reign within the diegesis, and names not connect signified and signifier, Dickens makes certain that his story retains its tightly woven meaning and even opens up occasional windows for readers alert enough to draw the threads together.

Sometimes it might appear that Dickens or his narrator has slipped up. Why, for example, would an author name his titular character Chuzzlewit? Such a name suggests an inferior, comic character—much more so than Pickwick, which is simply playful. Dickens did not come to the name easily, but considered several others, including Sweezlewag, Sweezlebach, Sweezleden, Chuzzletoe, and the favored Chuzzlewig. Only at the last stage did it become Chuzzlewit, certainly far the best of these names. But why such a pejorative name for the book's hero? The full early versions of the book's title provide the clue to an answer for they indicate that this is not merely the story of young Martin, but forms "a complete key to The House of chuz-zlewig" (Stone, Notes, 33). A glance at the novel's opening paragraph reveals that the so-called House of Chuzzlewit is the human race, which traces its heritage back to Adam and Eve. Hence, the Chuzzlewit family is all of us; we are all confused and selfish. And lest anyone think that this is a late inter-pretation, it is necessary only to observe that from Dickens's earliest notes for the novel, he wrote his intention that for the readers of this novel "Your homes the scene. Yourselves the actors here" (Stone, Notes, 31).

The power to name is enormously significant, though it also permits an illusion of command.[13] A notable example of this last instance is Pip in *Great Expectations,* who names himself by a slip of the tongue. This novel is also an interesting exception to the division between the nonnaming first-person and the naming third-person narrators of Dickens's novels. Pip is a notable example of the importance of naming, if for no other reason than that Dickens calls such attention to this speech act at the very outset of his novel, when his protagonist first becomes conscious of his own being. This sovereign speech act, however, is reported to us in the midst of much confu-sion on Pip's part, which includes his misunderstanding of what is written about his dead parents and siblings on their cemetery markers, and then the perturbation prompted by Magwitch's account of his bloodthirsty partner. It could be said that Pip has *misnamed* himself, since he has shrunk himself from the complete Philip Pirrip, to the diminutive Pip. From this point of view, one might conclude that Pip lives out his early career under a false name. As is frequently the case in Dickens's later fiction, he offers a redun-dancy of clues for the reader to grasp his full intentions, if not while reading, then when the reading is complete and all information is in. One such clue about Pip and names is in the brief episode when the young and still largely illiterate Pip writes a letter for Joe in which he shortens Joe's name to JO, an act of abbreviation resembling the shortening of his own name and hinting at his misvaluing of the man Joe as well, though interestingly, Joe can rec-ognize his name when he sees Pip's written JO, though he is otherwise no reader (75).

Appropriately, Pip's false name mirrors the falseness of his situation. His great expectations are to become a wealthy gentleman and Estella's husband, though in reality he will become an overseas merchant who is single when the narrative ends. Pip's misnaming of himself is thus consistent with the illusory life he leads through most of the narrative. By mistakenly assuming control of his own name, he loses command of his actual nature, accepting a form of secular destiny instead of forging his own fate. The verb "to forge" stems from the Old French *forgier,* derived from the Latin *fabricare,* to make or fashion. There are many modes of making, some true and some false, though *forge* suggests arduous creation. But to forge money is to be so false as to constitute criminality. Whereas Joe is true to the right purpose of forging, Pip forges an identity which he passes off as real in the world around him, despite the fact that several characters see through this specious form of specie, from Biddy to Trabb's boy to Dolge Orlick. The latter names Pip "wolf," a displacement of Pip's identity, but not inexplicable from the point of view of Orlick, to whom Pip has not been kind. There are many reasons for Pip's pervading sense of guilt and association with criminality, not the least of which is that he is living an alias. I am myself here playing with words to a specific end. The Forge is one of the most important place names in *Great Expectations*, and it carries the weight of many kinds of making because it is here that the core mystery of the plot is worked into shape, a fact that Dickens signals throughout the narrative by the recurring allusions to equipment associated with the Forge—a file, manacles, chains, and so forth.

Herbert Pocket changes Pip's name, preferring to call him Handel because of that musician's well-known composition "The Harmonious Blacksmith." A blacksmith is a man of physical power who can shape what is otherwise resistant to change through his mastery of the forge. Joe is true to the simple identity he did not make, but over which he takes control. Ceding domestic power to his wife is a sign of his real authority. Only those who hold power can lease it to others. No one offers to call Joe by anything but his given names. But by renaming Pip Handel, Herbert displaces Pip from his false identity without providing him with a true one, unlike the renamings of David Copperfield. Not he, but Dickens is calling attention to the parallel between Handel's translation of the rough work of the blacksmith into art and Pip's transformation from a blacksmith in fact into a role-playing gentleman. It is, after all, Herbert's father who has the task of coining this new gentleman. So Dickens's allusiveness, put in the mouth of Herbert as a thing of little significance, is actually a clue to the correct understanding of the entire novel. This name game comes full circle, when, near the close of the novel, we learn that Joe and Biddy's child has been named Pip. This will be his proper name and his proper identity to fulfill. The original Pip has presumably by this time achieved his true identity, which permits him to become the narrator of his own history; presumably he is now Philip Pirrip again and not that false construction known as Pip. Although, in Dickens's original ending of the novel, Estella calls Pip by that name, in the published ending, she does not.

Naming plays an important part throughout *Great Expectations*. Some names are neutral, as is Joe Gargery's. Others intend a comic sound, as with the guests gathered at the Gargery home—Wopsle, Hubble, and especially Pumblechook. Other names bear varying degrees of more intense meaning.

Abel Magwitch links an edenic name with suggestions of sorcery and wicked power.[14] Dolge Orlick, with its rolling vowels echoes the moroseness of its owner. Other names similarly play with sounds that are compatible with the characters they name, such as Drummle and Startop. A minor character is clearly skewered by being named Mrs. Coiler. But important characters are similarly well defined. Estella suggests a stellar inaccessibility, an apt name considering Dickens's initial ending of the novel, in which Pip does not attain his female prize. More evident is the meaning of Miss Havisham's name, for her entire life is a sham. These are necessary, but unoriginal observations. What is interesting to me is that Dickens in this novel gives Pip, a first-person narrator, a tendency to naming that resembles that of his third-person narrators. Pip the narrator has not named the characters mentioned above, but Pip the subject of the narration does rename Pepper, his unnecessary servant, as the Avenger. And something fairly complex is going on with the narrative when this happens. Pip the narrator has used many images of entanglement, such as golden chains, the reappearing file, and so forth to indicate a pattern of entrapment in Pip's career, but that is because he is narrating the account after the important events have transpired and have become a story that can be woven together with a clear teleological purpose. But Pip the subject of narration creates the minatory name for his servant while he is in the midst of that story, before it even is a story. Yet he fulfills Dickens's need to retain control of his narrative by putting in place the allusive and connotative blocks that constitute the edifice of his narrative. It is Dickens, too, who gives the narrating Pip his powers of metaphor.

Dickens exploits his naming game best in this novel with Jaggers and his clerk, Wemmick. While at first the two seem aptly paired—both secretive and solitary and devoted to the business of the law—, in fact, they are eventually distinguished from one another. Their names make this distinction precisely evident. Jaggers is as jagged and rough a name as one might wish for with its harsh vowels and consonants. Wemmick, by contrast, is almost a mellifluous name with its softened consonants. More intriguing is that the two names align perfectly, each consisting of seven letters with contrasting consonants and vowels matching exactly, a precise development of examples I gave earlier from *David Copperfield*. There is no accident in this kind of naming. Moreover, the place names associated with both men have a similar effect. Little Britain, though a real place, nonetheless has a spiky quality that makes it sound unattractive, whereas Walworth has a gentle, inviting tonality. These contrasting names, both of persons and of place, show what power Dickens could convey through his naming, for entire personalities and contexts are evoked in these names before any actions flesh them out. In some ways, they are Dickens's clues to his readers about how to receive each of his fictional personalities. We know before the secret is out that Wemmick is a better man than he seems. Walworth and Walworth sentiments are already implied in his name.

In her study of realism, *All Is True,* Lilian R. Furst identifies the eighteenth century as the period when location and actual place became important to fiction. Previously places bore symbolic and allegorical significance. "Only in the late eighteenth and early nineteenth centuries does fiction begin to develop environment as a matrix in which character is formed, and with this, the close articulation of places and people" (98). At the end of the eighteenth century, the romantic enthusiasm for landscape combines with curiosity about practical industrial matters and details of social organization. "The stark symbolism of allegory combines with the digressive prolixity of travel writing to produce the technique of detailed and cumulative notation of place normally associated with realism" (98). Furst notes that since Ian Watt's *The Rise of the Novel,* particularity of place has been considered a hallmark of realism. Because place names in fiction can and often do refer to real sites, they "can act as a bridge of continuity, along which readers may move from one sphere to the other without becoming conscious of the transition" (102). This easy flow between fiction and reality enhances the illusion of transparency to which realism aspires.

Here again, Dickens, though a master at particularity, does not employ his details for the same strategic ends as realism. Even with place names he often tries to evoke an emotional response, whether positive in a place like Dingley Dell, or negative, with the allegorically named Dotheboys Hall or Pocket Breaches, the town for which Veneering becomes a Member of Parliament. The first is readable even by a twenty-first century American student; the second requires some historical information. The name suggests a pocket borough—one controlled by a single individual or family, and hence a certainty for a favored parliamentary candidate. That such favor often involved cash payment is suggested by the name Dickens chose for the town, but even more by the names he listed in his mems, but then discarded—Ticklepocket and Twitchpocket.[15] If his characters exert or try to exert control over their environment and other characters through assuming the power to rename, Dickens himself overtly claims a similar authority through the reverberating significance of the names he gives to persons and things.[16] But Dickens also extends his own yen for naming places to his characters. Not many seriously realist novelists would have their characters offer place names such as Bleak House, Satis House, or the Golden Bower. But Dickens does not want to be a realist in the accepted sense of that term. Richard Lettis puts the matter well:

Above all, he thought that writing should enable the reader to see the essential affirmative 'truth' of life—this was for him the best that writing could achieve. He disliked the obvious, and approved always of subtlety, but knew that judicious use of the commonplace, of carefully-selected detail, could bring reality to a story—but it must always be the kind of reality he found in drama: 'wonderful reality'—the world as we know it, but 'polished by art' until it assumed values not felt in the dull settled world itself. For him reality was not what it was to the realists; it was neither commonplace as in Howells nor sordid as in so many others. (60–61)

I would add that Dickens wanted a wonderful reality not only polished by art, but specifically by the art of Charles Dickens.

When Dickens names a voting town Eatanswill, he is thumbing his nose at what was to become the realist convention because he wants his audience to be conscious of the author as a performer, as master of the sovereign act of naming.[17] When he confers that power upon his narrators and characters, he means to show his audience how important that power of naming is and how it remains ultimately the province of the author who is permitting his characters to name others and even themselves. But he also calls attention to the *sins* of naming in characters like Steerforth or Murdstone, and the *mistake* of naming in Pip. By telling the stories of those who do not understand how sovereign the act of naming is, Dickens reinforces his own power by using that act correctly and to its proper end.

CHAPTER 4

The Gentleman in the White Waistcoat

Dickens and Metonymy

ery early in *Oliver Twist*, Oliver makes the famous blunder of begging for more food, an offense which promptly brings him before the board of commissioners of the workhouse. When Bumble the beadle confirms that Oliver has asked for more after consuming the supper allotted by the dietary, "the man in the white waistcoat" declares: "'That boy will be hung ... I know that boy will be hung'" (11). Nobody controverts the man in the white waistcoat; Oliver is instantly confined and a notice is posted on the outside gate of the workhouse advertising his availability for apprenticeship to any trade. The gentleman in the white waistcoat asserts himself again. "'I never was more convinced of anything in my life,' said the gentleman in the white waistcoat, as he knocked at the gate and read the bill next morning: 'I never was more convinced of anything in my life, than I am, that that boy will come to be hung'" (12). This episode might have ended chapter 2, but the young Dickens does not drop the subject; instead, the narrator emphasizes his own relationship to the diegesis, linking his narrative task to the claims of the gentleman in the white waistcoat. "As I purpose to show in the sequel whether the whitewaistcoated gentleman was right or not, I should perhaps mar the interest of this narrative (supposing it to possess any at all), if I ventured to hint, just yet, whether the life of Oliver Twist had this violent termination or no" (37). Since the full title of Dickens's novel is *Oliver Twist, Or, The Parish Boy's Progress*, there is room for doubt about his ultimate fate. How much can be expected of a child born in a workhouse and brought up on the rates at the mercy of a penny-wise middle-class bureaucracy? Poverty and squalor are more likely to produce a criminal than a law-abiding citizen among any orphans who happen to survive the conditions of the workhouse. Oliver's fate might be that of Bulwer's Paul Clifford or Ainsworth's Jack Sheppard. Nonetheless, the narrator's obvious sympathy for Oliver from the outset makes it unlikely that he will progress to the gallows. Thus the narrator's coy positioning of himself in relation to the gentleman in the white waistcoat seems to constitute an opposition, not a conundrum. At this point in the narrative, the narrator already knows the general outcome of his narrative; the gentleman with the white waistcoat does not. He is simply confident that he does. Two unnamed individuals—the narrator and the man in the white waistcoat—present their forms of authority before their mutual audience, the novel's readers.

It might be argued that Dickens did not know the outcome of his narrative, given the haste with which he was writing several different texts at the same time that he was beginning *Twist*, but I would contend that, after *Pickwick*, he usually had his overall pattern in mind, even if he did not have the details of plot and character defined. An example of how he tended to think appears in a letter to Wilkie Collins, with whom he was writing "No Thoroughfare." He is concerned with the overall design first, which will culminate:

> in a wintry flight and pursuit across the Alps. Let us be obliged to go over— say the Simplon Pass—under lonely circumstances, and against warnings. Let us get into all the horrors and dangers of such an adventure under the most terrific circumstances, either escaping from, or trying to overtake (the latter, the better, I think) some one, on escaping from, or overtaking, whom, the love, prosperity, and Nemesis of the story depend. There we can get Ghostly interest, picturesque interest, breathless interest of time and circumstance, and force the design up to any powerful climax we please. (11:413)

But back to the man in the white waistcoat who has not finished his part in Oliver's drama. As chapter 3 begins, the narrator comments that, if the imprisoned Oliver had taken the gentleman with the white waistcoat's "sage advice," he would have hanged himself in his cell with his pocket handkerchief, except for the fact that, handkerchiefs being luxuries, workhouse boys have no access to them (12). This is an interesting proleptic moment, for a major part of the trade to which Fagin apprentices Oliver in London is the stealing of pocket handkerchiefs, potentially a hanging offense.[1] So this apparent aside has a resonance known only to the narrator. This is a secret bit of metonymy—the luxury of handkerchiefs equals crime—that prepares for a similar metonymy involving the white waistcoat. Moreover, the connection to Fagin is not accidental, for the man in the white waistcoat acts for Oliver much in the way the Artful Dodger does—as an agent for a potential employer. He encourages Gamfield the chimney sweep, "exactly the sort of master Oliver Twist wanted," to apply for the boy and even becomes his advocate, introducing him to the board of commissioners (14). Mr. Limbkin, the head of the board, realizes what a dangerous and revolting occupation chimney sweeping is for the boys who must climb up the flues and he expresses some sympathy along those lines, enough to drive a hard financial bargain with Gamfield. However, the sale of Oliver to the vile chimney sweep is prevented accidentally by a magistrate who is distracted from his doze and notices the terror in Oliver's face. He sends Oliver back to the workhouse with instructions that he be treated kindly. "That same evening," the narrator notes, "the gentleman in the white waistcoat most positively and decidedly affirmed, not only that Oliver would be hung, but that he would be drawn and quartered into the bargain" (19).

The gentleman in the white waistcoat appears to be one of those gratuitous items that occur in Dickens's narratives, which do not seem to have any integral function, but merely extend or enhance a given situation. The man in the white waistcoat might be an intensifier, since he not only endorses the board's treatment of Oliver, but seems to relish it with sadistic enjoyment. However, I suggest that the gentleman in the white waistcoat carries out a much more important function in the novel and is far from incidental, because he illustrates what I take to be a conscious narrative technique that Dickens employs to distance his work from what we normally identify as realist fiction. Moreover, I believe that Dickens understood the rules for what came to be recognized as realism and that he purposely violated them for his own ends.

In *Hidden Rivalries: Dickens, Realism and Revaluation*, Jerome Meckier places Dickens in the realist camp and argues that the major writers he examines—Dickens, Trollope, Gaskell, Eliot, Collins—were involved in a sly "realism war"; he declares that "the novelists themselves—professed realists all—read and reread one another," and then went on to overcome the version of realism of their competitors, most notably Dickens (2). Dickens had to respond in this war by reasserting his brand of realism in a constantly new way. But what I am suggesting is that Dickens's mode of evading the challenges of these contemporary rivals was to go *beyond* realism, to incorporate in his writings subversions of realism's stylistic assumptions to which they adhered. Many able critics, from John Romano's *Dickens and Reality* on, have argued pointedly that Dickens's fiction draws as much from romance, fairy tale, and allegory as it does from the mimetic tradition. Richard Lettis puts the situation well when he says that Dickens wanted a "wonderful reality" (see full quotation at the end of chapter 3 of this book). I have already indicated that Dickens held an attitude toward fiction shared by Bulwer-Lytton, which Edward Eigner describes as the metaphysical novel, an approach that stressed overall design before plot and characterization.

In a hostile evaluation of Dickens's career David Musselwhite depicts a Dickens who begins as a truly original narrator in the role of Boz, but transforms himself into a commodified author. He sees the anarchic, transparent world of Boz, along with some later passages, such as the description of Jacob's Island in *Oliver Twist* and of the Fleet Prison in *Pickwick* as preferable to the mannered prose of *Bleak House,* as in the description of New Bleak House.[2] The earlier work is impersonal and transparent in tone, whereas the later work is involved with the play of language itself, calling attention to itself. In a way, Musselwhite claims that Boz started as a realist and Dickens turned into a nonrealist, whatever we want to call that other entity. But again, my argument here is that Dickens became increasingly aware of how the various tropes of narration operated in what we call realism and he did not wish to be contained within those limits. Moreover, there are many moments in Boz's *Sketches* where Dickens has already grasped this notion. J. Hillis Miller showed in "*Sketches by Boz, Oliver Twist,* and Cruikshank's Illustrations," that what critics and readers had so long accepted as precise reportage in the *Sketches* must be read in a different way. "The Sketches are not mimesis of an externally existing reality, but the interpretation of that reality according to highly artificial schemas inherited from the past" (32). And again: "The metonymic associations which Boz makes are fancies rather than facts, impositions on the signs he sees of stock conventions, not mirroring but interpretations, which is to say lies" (35). Miller indicates that Dickens was at least partially conscious of his own methods in the way he organized the *Sketches* for book publication. "The movement from Scene to Character to Tale is not the metonymic process authenticating realistic representation but a movement deeper and deeper into the conventional, the concocted, the schematic" (35).

What happens as Dickens matures as a writer is that he does become more conscious of the play of language itself because he learns to use language in craftier ways. To recognize the double edge of metonymy, for example, provides him with a powerful tool not merely for narration, but for complexity of theme. To connect patterns of metonymy over whole novels is to raise his narrative from simple realism to a style that prefigures the leitmotif technique of Richard Wagner in music, or Thomas Mann's application of that technique to fiction, perhaps most self-consciously in *Doctor Faustus*. Musselwhite complains that in his description of Carker's room in *Dombey and Son* Dickens has moved away from surfaces and textures toward a concentration on inner malignity and thus heavily loads its details against Carker. But that is the point! Plain realism could describe the room and associate certain objects with malign intent, let us say, but Dickens goes beyond that to characterize the objects as metonymic of Carker's *inner* condition. It is the *reverse* of what the realist seeks to accomplish.

I cannot here go into detail about the mimetic tradition. It is possible to discuss Dickens's departure from that tradition in several ways, as I hope this study shows, but, for the purposes of this chapter, I would like to focus on one aspect of realism that seems to have received general agreement among critics over the years. That is the connection of metonymy with realist technique. Because metonymy is important in defining realism, I intend to show that Dickens used this trope in a manner contrary to its customary use in realist writing. Roman Jakobson formulated this identification of metonymy with realism when he opposed it to metaphor, which he allied to poetry. He wrote:

> The primacy of the metaphoric process in the literary schools of romanticism and symbolism has been repeatedly acknowledged, but it is still insufficiently realized that it is the predominance of metonymy which underlies and actually predetermines the so-called 'realistic' trend, which belongs to an intermediary stage between the decline of romanticism and the rise of symbolism and is opposed to both. Following the path of contiguous relationships, the realistic author metonymically digresses from the plot to the atmosphere and from the characters to the setting in space and time. He is fond of synechdochic details. (77–78)[3]

Virginia Woolf in her own way had already established the linkage of metonymy and realism in "Mr. Bennett and Mrs. Brown," with the purpose of showing its limitations. She divides up the writers of her day into Edwardians and Georgians, the former representing the realism of the past, the latter the modernism of the future. Bennett is one of the former, whose tools, Woolf says, no longer work for the present generation. The chief of these tools was elaborate description, so that character could be determined by what the human being was associated with among inanimate things. She concludes:

That is what I mean by saying that the Edwardian tools are the wrong ones for us to use. They have laid an enormous stress upon the fabric of things. They have given us a house in the hope that we may be able to deduce the human beings who live there. To give them their due, they have made that house much better worth living in. But if you hold that novels are in the first place about people, and only in the second about the houses they live in, that is the wrong way to set about it. (332)

Recently, Harry Shaw has examined the history of this relationship in some detail. He accepts Jakobson's ordering of metonymy with realism, but extends the idea along his own lines.

To the extent, then, that we imagine ourselves back into a situation in which we can take seriously the claims of figural realism to capture the real, we find ourselves conceiving of the connections it makes as metonymical in nature. After Dante, figural realism appears to be founded in a species of metaphor—as does much of the literature we most prize. But that is because our culture's sense of the real has itself shifted. I draw from this the following moral, which extends Jakobson's contention that metonymy is the trope characteristic of nineteenth-century prose fiction: the defining trope of all realisms is metonymy—but it is metonymy as defined in the light of the ontology to which a given realism appeals.
    If we return to our model of realism, then, I am suggesting that the mechanism that connects different levels in modern realism is a historicist metonymy. This metonymy assumes as many inflections as there are realist novelists. (103–4)

Without offering any particulars, Shaw excludes Dickens from his study, as I see it, correctly.
    There are many ways in which realism does not and cannot conform to its own largely unwritten rules. Bruce Robbins has shown, for example, that British realism scarcely represents an entire part of the population. There are few significant representatives of "the people" in this literature, and, ironically, when "the people" are represented, it is servants, dependents within the households and thus extensions of their masters, who stand in for the lower classes. Robbins claims that servants are not even depicted as genuine representatives of their historical context, but fulfill roles that existed in the earliest sources of Western literature, such as Greek drama. Servants thus serve an almost symbolic role in representing the rebellious, resistant, and otherwise challenging forces arrayed against the master class. For the most part, Robbins argues, realist novelists did not try to offer a genuine picture

of the lower classes, but fell back upon a trusty convention. In a more recent study, Katherine Kearns argues that realism surreptitiously and unconsciously evokes those elements of experience that it seeks to repress. She has several different formulations of this idea, but here is one. "Realism's doubled intuitions for the social and the ineffable ensure both that the sublime will make itself attractive and that its attractions will be appropriately chastised; one ends up with authorial gestures that simultaneously acknowledge and repudiate the seductions of the sublime" (114). Many other studies indicate various qualifications of realism's claims to true mimesis.

In a similar fashion, critics writing specifically on Dickens have examined ways in which his narratives must be seen as standing to one side of the realist tradition. A recent example is Juliet John's *Dickens's Villains: Melodrama, Character, Popular Culture*, which argues that the flatness of Dickens's characters is intentional. Dickens is not aiming primarily at the examination of internal states of mind, but wishes to show that his characters are part of a larger community. Interiority is thus hostile to the communal drive of his narratives, and is therefore associated primarily with villains and their like, a practice inherited from the stage, especially in its melodramatic modes.

My claim here, then, is not that I am making an original observation when I say that Dickens should not be placed within the mainstream realist tradition, if such a thing really exists, but that he appropriated devices associated with realism and used them to ends that operate against the realist program. Again, I do not mean to say that he defined himself against realism, but that by hindsight we can recognize that he was resisting a mode of representation which came to dominance in fiction during his lifetime, fueled largely by the popularity of Sir Walter Scott's fiction, though Scott himself was not a realist. Throughout this book I examine different ways in which Dickens sets himself against or outside of realist practice, but here I shall concentrate on the one feature of metonymy, and that returns us to the issue of the gentleman in the white waistcoat in *Oliver Twist*.

I have chosen the gentleman in the white waistcoat as my example because he is so rudimentary and he appears so early in Dickens's career. Dickens used metonymic devices brilliantly in his earliest writings. "Reflections in Monmouth Street" is an example, where, beginning with the old clothes exhibited in a ragshop, the narrator constructs from their appearance the lives of their former owners.[4] The clothes bear the traces of a former life. Of course, this is the reverse of how metonymy usually works, where an article of clothing might indicate a person's function. A prominent example is the scene in Hardy's *Far from the Madding Crowd* where Gabriel Oak goes to the market to find work as a farm agent only to encounter employers seeking shepherds instead. Oak identifies himself as a potential agent by wearing middle-class clothing, but changes to his shepherd's smock, hoping to find a place as a shepherd through this new identifying attire, only ironically to be passed over by an employer who is looking for an agent. Clothes mark the man.

The gentleman in the white waistcoat is interesting because he remains nameless and is identified chiefly by this one article of clothing and by his vicious sentiments. This is all the more striking since Dickens had declared in *Sketches by Boz* that viewing the exterior of a person was a surer guarantee of comprehending his character than written description can provide, thus to offer almost no description at all must be seen not as a disclaimer (as it is in the *Sketches,* where Boz amusingly goes on to provide the description he says is unnecessary), but as a conscious strategy (*Sketches* 158–59). The gentleman in *Oliver* is thus entirely surface to us. We get no physical description of him as we do of Gamfield in detail to indicate *his* viciousness. We have just that white waistcoat as a token of his identity. Does the whiteness of the waistcoat signify anything, let us say, like the whiteness of Moby Dick, where Melville's narrator himself opens whiteness to multiple interpretations? Let us begin with the social significance of the waistcoat.

Dickens knew about waistcoats and, in his early manhood favored elaborate examples. C. Willett Cunnington and Phillis Cunnington in their *Handbook of English Costume in the Nineteenth Century* note that in the 1820s and 1830s the waistcoat had become quite dramatic, with dandies wearing all colors of the rainbow. They remark that the waistcoat "had become the most striking male garment; a gentleman's inventory of 1828 revealed 36 white waistcoats costing £54" (104). One might assume that, though this gentleman had white waistcoats, they were not necessarily plain, since many waistcoats described as white were of elegant fabrics, such as silk or satin. In the early part of the century a white satin embroidered waistcoat with gold thread was a standard article of Court dress. The Exquisites of the 1830s wore white waistcoats with elaborate costumes. Here are two examples quoted by the Cunningtons from magazines of the time.

"In a light brown coat, white waistcoat, nankin pantaloons buttoned at the ankle with two gold buttons, yellow stockings with large violet clocks, shoes with buckles of polished cut steel."

". . . with green coat, broad velvet collar, white waistcoat, pantaloons of glazed white ticking tight to the knees." (107)

Anne Buck points out that waistcoats, where "[m]ost of the colour and ornament of men's dress was concentrated," often "showed the fabrics and colours and woven and printed designs fashionable in the materials of women's dress" (188). Many of the waistcoats that survive from the nineteenth century were wedding waistcoats often "in white or cream figured silk, or white silk embroidered" (188).

It seems, then, that white waistcoats were quite a common feature of men's dress both for formal occasions, such as weddings and Court appearances, and for ordinary use. Apparently a great deal depended upon the materials out of which these waistcoats were fashioned and the cut of their design. But Dickens tells us nothing more about the man in the white waistcoat's waistcoat except that it is white. The whole man thus depends upon this overwhelmingly identifying physical object and his dialogue, or nearly so. But I shall return to that in a minute. First I want to indicate that this trait in Dickens's method of characterization stayed with him throughout his career and took on interesting variations. I shall mention just a couple of instances here because my space is limited. In *Little Dorrit,* Merdle is intimidated by his butler, who is a grave and sober man, far more refined than his master. It is in Merdle's interest to demonstrate to society all the trappings of wealth and high social status.

> The chief butler was the next magnificent institution of the day. He was the stateliest man in company. He did nothing, but he looked on as few other men could have done. He was Mr. Merdle's last gift to Society. Mr. Merdle didn't want him, and was put out of countenance when the great creature looked at him; but inappeasable Society would have him—and had got him. (243–44)

To this point, what we apparently have is some sharp social satire. Merdle's inferiority to his own servant makes a mockery of his supposed power. The butler should metonymically serve as a manifestation of the household to accomplish realist ends. And he does, except that in this case he does so ironically. So it would appear that this brief passage fulfills a realist purpose, though any reader should be wary of so quickly accepting it in that way, since it occurs in a chapter where the guests at Merdle's home are named as Treasury, Bar, and Bishop and fulfill typical, not individual, functions. Later we encounter Merdle wandering through his great house with "no apparent object but escape from the presence of the chief butler" (386). And a few lines later we are introduced to his habit of "clasping his wrists as if he were taking himself into custody" (386). Soon the "chief butler" becomes the "Chief Butler" and is described as "the Avenging Spirit of this great man's life" (540).

Something similar happens in *Great Expectations* when Pip, feeling the need to confirm his status as a gentleman, hires an unneeded servant whose name is Pepper. In what might be mistaken as the typical metonymic device of associating character and social rank with clothing, Pip begins, "I had got so fast of late, that I had even started a boy in boots," signifying that the boy's status as a servant is indicated by his livery, which Pip goes on to describe—"and had clothed him with a blue coat, canary waistcoat, white cravat, creamy breeches, and the boots already mentioned" (210). The boy, however, is as much a nuisance as a help and to indicate this Pip employs a language already strongly thematic throughout the novel. He says that he is "in bondage and slavery" after he has "made this monster" (210). Since Pip later alludes to the Frankenstein creature, it is possible to link this reference to the later motif of the creature's avenging pursuit of Victor Frankenstein. Hence, what begins with a "realist" ploy quickly evolves into a symbolic function. Seeing Pepper as an "avenging phantom," he renames him the Avenger, and before long this function, which is a product of Pip's imagination and has nothing to do with the boy's own nature or conduct, becomes the major and metonymic way of referring to him. But he is no longer metonymically connected to the social world; he is now a part of Pip's internal realm which is peopled with images of convicts, chains of gold, punishment, revenge, and so forth. I need not catalog the well-known web of such references that make this novel such densely rich reading. The metonym in this very simple instance consciously transfers Pepper out of the range of servant-and-master social relations and into a symbolic range of references operating against the realist agenda. Metonym blends with metaphor and even suggests allegorical dimensions.

Late in his career, Dickens is able to turn this kind of trope into a brand of shorthand that blurs the difference between metaphor/simile and metonym. For convenience sake, I will use an example that almost reprises the instance of the butler above. At the Veneerings' house in *Our Mutual Friend,* we again have generic figures Boots and Brewer and an ominous servant, this time a retainer who "goes round, like a gloomy Analytical Chemist; always seeming to say, after 'Chablis, sir?'—'You wouldn't if you knew what it's made of'" (10). By his next appearance and thereafter the simile disappears. Moreover, the gloom identified with him is transferred to those he serves, thus we see Eugene Wrayburn "gloomily resorting to the champagne chalice whenever proferred by the Analytical Chemist" (11). In his next appearance, he has become simply "the Analytical" (250). And this shift emphasizes a feature of the character that proves significant and fits him into the tenor of the novel as a whole.[5] This apparently insignificant individual is capable of analyzing the situation around him accurately. In this novel crammed with secrets and mysteries, only a few individuals have this power of penetration and yet it is precisely this penetration that the narrator offers, especially in relationship to seeing past the surface of the Veneerings. Just as he knows better than others what the constituents of the chablis are, the Analytical is equally acute about other domestic features. When Mrs. Veneering reports that Baby was uneasy in her sleep on the night of the election that will give Mr. Veneering a seat in Parliament, "The Analytical chemist, who is gloomily looking on, has diabolical impulses to suggest 'Wind' and throw up his situation; but represses them" (253–54). In his last appearance, the Analytical Chemist feels he could give Veneering an apt answer to the question: How do people live beyond their means? In his brief moments on stage he has become more and more judgmental, so it is not surprising that he departs the text as "the Analytical, perusing a scrap of paper lying on the salver, with the air of a literary Censor . . ." (627). It might be said that Dickens here discloses his affiliation with this subversive character.

What is significant for the purposes of this essay is that Dickens calls attention to his nonrealist joke on metonymy. A household servant is unlikely to have a metonymic connection with the science of chemistry. By converting a servant to an Analytical Chemist, Dickens aligns the servant with "scientific" analysis, something carried out methodically elsewhere in the novel by the police and others. The servant is a tiny image of the potential disclosure of untrue conditions that mirrors the effort of the novel as a whole. At his last appearance the Analytical Chemist has returned to simile, only now it is as the Analytical Chemist, not as a household retainer, that he is likened to a "literary Censor." This simile marks him as a literary artifact, thus marking him a product of fancy rather than fact, and indicating that he has never been a participant in a "real" domain, but a figure highjacked out of allegory. He becomes a sign pointing to a particular function of the narrative and thus resembles the allegorical figure on the ceiling of Tulkinghorn's room with his ominous pointing hand. This technique can operate in the reverse direction as well, as a simple example from *A Christmas Carol* shows.

Near the opening of the story, the narrator asserts that "Old Marley was as dead as a door-nail" and then boldly calls our attention to the figurative expression. "Mind! I don't mean to say that I know, of my own knowledge, what there is particularly dead about a door-nail. I might have been inclined, myself, to regard a coffin-nail as the deadest piece of ironmongery in the trade" (7). This bit of self-conscious playfulness about the narrator's own language might have ended right here, but it is actually preparation for a far more important episode. When Scrooge arrives at his house that evening, he finds on his door, "not a knocker, but Marley's face" (15). The ironmongery simile that proved Marley dead now becomes an ironmongery that shows him not entirely dead at all. From being a dead character, Marley has become a real presence to Scrooge. More ironmongery follows. The bells in the house begin to chime on their own, introducing the appearance of Marley's ghost wearing a chain made "of cash-boxes, keys, padlocks, ledgers, deeds, and heavy purses wrought in steel" (17). Marley explains his bizarre ornament.

> "I wear the chain I forged in life," replied the Ghost. "I made it link by link, and yard by yard; I girded it on of my own free will, and of my own free will I wore it. Is its pattern strange to you?" (19)

Marley's chosen attitude toward life has constituted this punishment in the hereafter, and Scrooge has been forging his own similar chain. By now the simple simile of ironmongery has become a forbidding symbolism. The metonymic items of Marley's business have been transmuted into a nearly allegorical object—an iron chain.

What is happening in *Oliver Twist* is simpler, but depends upon the same irony that operates in the other examples I have cited. It is important that the narrator almost always refers to the man as the *gentleman* in the white waistcoat (his first reference is the exception). There is no doubt about his status, but the repetition of this word, always linked to the white waistcoat reinforces his social place as one that is privileged. To some degree, then, the gentleman in the white waistcoat is a counter for a whole class. It would be possible to provide a sociological analysis, indicating that only a gentleman comfortably well off could afford such a fashionable item which would require expensive laundering and so forth. White gloves similarly indicated station through the implication that they would have to be changed during the day and many of them laundered over time. Thus articles of clothing encode a certain social attitude and even ideology. But that kind of analysis is not my purpose here. I am concerned here with Dickens's style rather than his politics. The man in the white waistcoat is not most importantly a representative of his class, but a peculiarly malign specimen. His prejudices completely overwhelm him. Oliver comes before the workhouse board, which consists of "eight or ten fat gentlemen . . . sitting around a table" (8). He is asked his name and hesitates to answer, being intimidated by so many gentlemen. The gentleman in a white waistcoat intervenes with an outburst that Oliver "was a fool. Which was a capital way of raising his spirits, and putting him quite at his ease" (9). There is a great deal of obvious irony in this scene at the expense of the gentlemen. For example, this famous passage: "The members of this board were very sage, deep, philosophical men; and when they came to turn their attention to the workhouse, they found out at once, what ordinary folks would never have discovered—the poor people liked it!" (9–10). But the gentleman in the white waistcoat is not merely stupid in this manner; he has a determined animus against the poor. He does not merely assume the worst about the poor, but wishes them ill. The head of the board instructs Oliver, but the gentleman in the white waistcoat adds his own view immediately after.

> "Well! You have come here to be educated, and taught a useful trade," said the red-faced gentleman in the high chair.
> "So you'll begin to pick oakum to-morrow morning at six o'clock," added the surly one in the white waistcoat. (9)

This unexplained, gratuitous nastiness sums up the gentleman in the white waistcoat and raises him almost to the level of symbolic representation. In some ways we *are* faced with the mystery of whiteness similar to that in *Moby-Dick*.

Near the beginning of this chapter, I noted the narrative irony of the narrator's comment on the handkerchief that Oliver could not have hanged himself with because handkerchiefs were a luxury in the workhouse, and I suggested that this reference is the narrator's proleptic joke, because handkerchiefs will play an important role in Oliver's subsequent career. One prominent connection has to do with hanging, so that the gentleman in the white waistcoat is actually the first to voice a motif that proliferates through the text in a manner that becomes typical of Dickens's style, of which I have tried to give a few brief examples from other novels above. Since Dickens was writing under great pressure while composing *Oliver Twist,* it cannot be assumed that he planned out that intricate pattern of handkerchief references, but it can be assumed that his imagination instinctively worked in this way. In later writings, it is clear that he consciously employs the technique.

Earlier I quoted from Katherine Kearns's *Nineteenth-Century Literary Realism: Through the Looking-Glass.* One chapter in this book is entitled "A Tropology of Realism in *Hard Times.*" It is a very intriguing and valuable reading of Dickens's novel. At one point Kearns summarizes her perception of Dickens's dilemma—how *Hard Times* presents double messages at every level of its discourses, reflecting Dickens's anxiety about and his resistance to the realistic mode.

> His apprehension of some alternative and unnameable energy brings his metonymies to challenge their own directional, propagandistic contiguities; people, their characters formed in some secret place, seem as much to create or to alter their surroundings as to be created or altered by them. (188)

Kearns is acute in noting the ways in which metonymy works in this novel.

She sees that "the language that reveals character through metonymy in *Hard Times* must communicate Coketown's essential nature as a fabricated construct, its strangeness only masked by the conventional linearities of its architecture . . ." (190). And she demonstrates that Bounderby's character, though dependent upon metonymies, refutes itself with its past, thus resisting the realistic program of the novel, for he is not what he is; his character has nothing to do with his past and thus is not explicable in terms of his own current realism. I couldn't agree more, but Kearns seems to feel that Dickens brings about this disjunction inadvertently, that he is unconsciously subverting his own attempt at realism.[6] It seems to me more sensible to regard Dickens as intentionally bringing about exactly these deconstructions. After all, he is attacking the Utilitarian materiality represented by the Gradgrinds and Bounderbys and he means to demonstrate its falseness. It is spectacularly evident that Bounderby, the enemy of fancy, is himself the most fanciful storyteller in the novel, having fabricated his entire early history. My argument is that Dickens employed metonymy in his fiction precisely to call attention to that part of experience that is not limited to materiality. He made his inclinations clear in his famous preface to *Bleak House* when he wrote: "In Bleak House, I have purposely dwelt upon the romantic side of familiar things" (xiv).

In *Hard Times,* Dickens aggressively calls attention to the difference between the metonymic and the metaphoric, the "realistic" and the "fanciful," in his style. At the very opening of the story Mr. Gradgrind is described as having a "square wall of a forehead, which had his eyebrows for its base, while his eyes found commodious cellarage in two dark caves, overshadowed by the wall" (1). The square wall connects Gradgrind metonymically with the business/industry, no-nonsense aspect of Coketown. But the eyes in their cave associate him metaphorically with a different pattern in the novel that has to do with redemptive danger and with the capacity to imagine beyond the factual and the material. Kearns has called attention to the way in which the square wall pattern proliferates as the narrative proceeds.

> Thus Gradgrind's "own metallurgical Louisa" is most literally a metonymic chip off the old block who lives in Stone Lodge, having been struck off the parent with a piece of the thing that names her; the implied syntagmatic progression goes nicely from the obdurate industrialism embodied in Coketown's red-brick buildings to Stone Lodge to the wall- and warehouse-like Mr. Gradgrind to his flinty offspring. (187–88)

That is the metonymic development of the square wall, but the metaphoric development of the dark caves is equally complex and pervasive, though perhaps even subtler. It finds expression in the "ditch" that Bounderby claims to have been born in as well as in the "dark pit of shame and ruin at the bottom" of the mighty staircase Mrs. Sparsit imagines Louisa descending, and in the uncovered shaft into which Stephen Blackpool falls. The ditch is the product of Bounderby's imagination, not a reality; the pit is the product of Mrs. Sparsit's imagination, and never becomes real; the shaft, though real enough, is the medium through which Stephen Blackpool, by the power of his positive imagination, conceives the central truth of the novel. While lying in the mineshaft he can see a star in the sky. "'I thowt it were the star as guided to Our Saviour's home. I awmust think it be the very star!'" The narrator endorses Stephen's perception. "The star had shown him where to find the God of the poor; and through humility, and sorrow, and forgiveness, he had gone to his Redeemer's rest" (274).

This tendency to take a small detail from early in the narrative and elaborate it in an increasing network of allusions and similarities is typical of Dickens's narrative method and is related to the examples I have given in the narrator's mention of a handkerchief early in *Oliver Twist*, the butler in *Little Dorrit*, and Pepper in *Great Expectations*. Dickens does not disguise his purpose and his method from any careful reader. Even as McChoakumchild (and the name gives away the narrator's moral alignment) is calling for the schoolchildren to be filled with facts, the narrator obstinately contains his efforts within the realm of fancy.

> He went to work in this preparatory lesson, not unlike Morgiana in the Forty Thieves: looking into all the vessels ranged before him, one after another, to see what they contained. Say, good McChoakumchild. When from thy boiling store, thou shalt fill each jar brimfull by-and-by, dost thou think that thou wilt always kill outright the robber Fancy lurking within—or sometimes only maim him and distort him! (8)

This is throwing down the gauntlet, as the shift to preacherly diction directly suggests. But if the narrator confines his Utilitarian characters within the circle of well-known fable, he does so in order to counteract a similar action perpetrated by these characters themselves. Here is what we learn of the young Gradgrinds, brought up through their father's fact-based training.

> The first object with which they had an association or of which they had a remembrance, was a large black-board with a dry Ogre chalking ghastly white figures on it.
>
> Not that they knew, by name or nature, anything about an Ogre. Fact forbid! I only use the word to express a monster in a lecturing castle, with

Heaven knows how many heads manipulated into one, taking childhood captive, and dragging it into gloomy statistical dens by the hair. (19)

This reads like a parody of the Giant Despair in *Pilgrim's Progress*—one of the all-time great fictions illustrating the positive power of fancy—who captures and confines Christian and Hopeful in a dungeon because they have strayed out of the true way. Here, however, the children are innocent captives and the den into which they are drawn bears a family resemblance to the caves of Gradgrind's eyes and the other ditches, pits, shafts, and so forth that emerge as the narrative proceeds, culminating in Stephen's release from his chasm into the freedom of death. In the contest between metonymy and metaphor, metaphor wins, but metonymy has also been drafted to the work of symbolic architecture which subverts and transcends what we call realism. J. Hillis Miller points out the way in which metonymy in Dickens crosses the line from its realistic function. He writes: "The metonymic reciprocity between a person and his surroundings, his clothes, furniture, house, and so on, is the basis for the metaphorical substitutions so frequent in Dickens's fiction. For Dickens, metonymy is the foundation and support of metaphor" (13).[7] In *Hard Times* the work of subversion is planned, open, and direct, whereas in *Oliver Twist,* for example, it seems largely instinctive. Nonetheless, as early as *Twist,* Dickens was willing to deliver a sly clue to his purposes. After the opening chapters, the gentleman in the white waistcoat disappears from the narrative. But in chapter 51, as the story is drawing to a close, Dickens makes what seems to be an entirely gratuitous move when he has Mr. Bumble remark to Oliver, "'Master Oliver, my dear, you remember the blessed gentleman in the white waistcoat? Ah! He went to heaven last week, in a oak coffin with plated handles, Oliver'" (345). Bumble by this time has been totally discredited, and so his statement here can be read as just the opposite of what he says. The gentleman was scarcely "blessed" and is not likely to have gone to heaven, given his uncharitable temperament. The oak coffin with plated handles constitutes more of the trappings of gentility, of a piece with the white waistcoat. This is the narrator (and Dickens, we can assume) dealing a little bit of poetic justice, just before the more commanding instances of the deaths of Fagin and Sikes. Nonetheless, it is Dickens revealing a sample of his handiwork.

In the realist tradition, metonymic connections help to identify characters with social place, occupation, and mental or emotional ability. The details might be articles of clothing, tools, and so forth, but these articles are subordinate to the purpose of making sharper the nature of the human figure. For realism, metonymy reinforces materiality. By contrast, in *Oliver Twist,* Dickens uses a repetitive metonymy to obliterate any specific human identity and makes his gentleman in the white waistcoat instead the embodiment of a malign spirit, dispersing the materiality of the individual man into a class atmospheric. Realism is not supposed to take this leap, though, in fact, a number of supposed realists could not resist such moves at one time or another. But Dickens makes this a regular practice in his writing and seems to be doing so in resistance to the growing impulse in the writing of his time to favor elaborate examinations of internal states partly through metonymic connections, preferring instead to represent a world with symbolic overtones, no matter how deeply he was capable of giving the impression of rooting it in a palpable reality.

CHAPTER 5

Dickens and Personification

eorge Ford wrote that at the height of Dickens's career, there was a general growing appreciation of the esthetics of fiction along with a growing demand for realism in the novel, which created a tendency for critics to misvalue the developments in Dickens's own writing (128). Though Dickens employed many nonrealist techniques, one feature of his writing that might have been off-putting for a critic demanding greater realism was his frequent use of personification. What figurative device is less conducive to realism than personification, so deeply connected to unrealistic genres such as allegory and fable? Although Dickens was fully aware of his fanciful use of personification in his fiction, he also used the device frequently in his personal discourse.

This tendency surfaces early in Dickens's career, sometimes with amusing irony. Referring to an essay for *Bentley's Miscellany*, Dickens wrote to Theodore Martin, "The Dying Student is also at the Printer's. I will look him up, and entomb him in the February number" (*Letters* I, 479). The personification of a piece of writing is not remarkably original, but to transform publication into entombment is. Rodney Stenning Edgecombe has examined personification in Dickens, but his approach is to discuss abstractions made concrete, such as Mendicity. He also makes an interesting observation about how alert Dickens was to the whole idea of personification, by pointing out that Dickens converts an idle personification—the allegory of the pointing Roman on Tulkinghorn's ceiling in *Bleak House*—to a functional one (232–33).

In this chapter, however, I emphasize the animating quality of personification and am not interested in locutions such as "blind justice," which offer embodiments of abstractions, or "Heep was the personification of guile," which offers an individual as an abstract model. Instead, I shall demonstrate that Dickens combines personification and deanimation as companion devices to emphasize the way in which human existence may be perceived as hyperreal, hence constituting an implied resistance to the realist movement, for which personification was not an acceptable tool. That his tendency to this form of personification was part of Dickens's worldview is evident in some of his public statements. In an address at a banquet in his honor at Hartford on February 7, 1842, he stated his belief that nothing is high because it is in a high place, and that nothing is low because it is in a low one, and then added:

> This is a lesson taught us in the great book of nature. This is the lesson which may be read, alike in the bright track of the stars, and in the dusty course of the poorest thing that drags its tiny length upon the ground. This is the lesson ever uppermost in the thoughts of that inspired man, who tells us that there are
>
> Tongues in trees, books in the running brooks,
> Sermons in stones, and good in everything. (*Speeches* 24)

For Dickens, all of existence, both animate and inanimate, contained a kind of spirit that the human imagination could release. Dorothy Van Ghent notably called attention to this practice in "The Dickens World: A View from Todgers's," stating that "[t]he course of things demonically possessed is to imitate the human, while the course of human possession is to imitate the inhuman" (213). She stresses, as I do, not only the animation of the inanimate, but the deanimating of the living. She offers many examples, of which the following is one instance. "Those who have engaged, as Grandfather Smallweed has, in the manipulation of their fellows as if they were things, themselves develop thing-attributes, like Podsnap, the capitalist, who has hair-brushes on his head instead of hair . . ." (214). Raymond Williams also notes that "the characteristics of houses and of people are consciously exchanged" in Dickens's fiction, providing "a way of seeing the city as a destructive animal" (159). Harvey Peter Sucksmith states that animism and a sense of force permeating things is typical of introverted vision, which he argues is part of Dickens's makeup (345). This may be so, but my claim here is that Dickens consciously employed the device of personification or animation to create a literature that feels free to exceed the limits of realism and to stimulate a similar kind of animating activity in his readers.[1]

An early and simple instance of my sense of personification occurs in *The Pickwick Papers.* I choose this particular example because it combines humans, other living creatures, and inanimate things all contained in one modal presentation.

> The morning which broke upon Mr. Pickwick's sight, at eight o'clock, was not at all calculated to elevate his spirits, or to lessen the depression which the unlooked-for result of his embassy inspired. The sky was dark and gloomy, the air was damp and raw, the streets were wet and sloppy. The smoke hung sluggishly above the chimney-tops as if it lacked the courage to rise, and the rain came slowly and doggedly down, as if it had not even the spirit to pour. A game-cock in the stable-yard, deprived of every spark of his accustomed animation, balanced himself dismally on one leg in a corner; a donkey, moping with drooping head under the narrow roof of an outhouse, appeared from his meditative and miserable countenance to be contemplating suicide. In the street, umbrellas were the only things to be seen, and the clicking of pattens and splashing of rain-drops, were the only sounds to be heard. (713)

In this passage, which opens chapter 51, Dickens starts us out with his central character, noting his depressed mood. He then proceeds to an ordinary description of the weather, but soon modulates into a projection of human agency onto smoke and rain, though this agency appropriately mirrors Mr. Pickwick's gloomy mood. Having thus animated smoke and rain, he turns to animals, attributing to them similar bad human moods, with the alarming prospect of the donkey considering suicide. Having taken us to this extreme point, Dickens returns to straightforward description, with the forceful detail of the clicking pattens. While seeming to be a description of the day, the passage is actually an improvisation on Mr. Pickwick's subjective state. This extending of a human mood to the nonhuman world is a technique that Dickens used throughout his career, often in his descriptions of buildings, whose windows are blind eyes, and who must sometimes, as in *Little Dorrit,* lean on crutches to support themselves. The technique, even with the moderating "as ifs," is one that calls attention to the way in which humans construct the world around them according to their moods, a perception that Dickens inherited from the Romantic writers who had called attention to the positive, restorative aspects of this human tendency, but also to its negative qualities. Drawing upon John Ruskin, the New Critics referred to this tendency as the Pathetic Fallacy. It would be frowned upon in realistic writing.

I believe that Dickens was well aware of what he was doing and was able to amuse himself with the idea. An extreme example of such play, also from *Pickwick,* occurs not as a mere figure of speech, but as a core part of plot. In chapter 14, a bagman tells the story of Tom Smart, who stops at a country inn and takes a fancy to the widow who owns it, though she is already apparently being courted by "a tall man—a very tall man—in a brown coat and bright basket buttons, and black whiskers, and wavy black hair . . ." (181). Tom thinks how nice it would be to marry the widow and become owner of the inn while he is having five tumblers of hot punch before retiring to bed. In his room, Tom is particularly struck by "a strange, grim-looking high-backed chair" with "legs carefully tied up in red cloth, as if it had got the gout in its toes" (183). This description already hints at personification, for the chair has traces of character in the opening adjectives, and the reference to its possible gout intensifies the tendency. Later, Tom awakes from a dream and immediately focuses on the chair again. He tries to go back to sleep, but can only see chairs dancing before his eyes, so he opens them. And now something peculiar indeed occurs.

> Tom gazed at the chair; and, suddenly as he looked at it, a most extraordinary change seemed to come over it. The carving of the back gradually assumed the lineaments and expression of an old shrivelled human face; the damask cushion became an antique, flapped waistcoat; the round knobs grew into a couple of feet, encased in red cloth slippers; and the old chair looked like a very ugly old man, of the previous century, with his arms akimbo. (183–84)

Here is personification with a vengeance! What's more, Tom actually engages in conversation with the chair, which comes around to the subject of the landlady, the chair remarking on her attractions. "Here the old fellow screwed up his eyes, cocked up one of his wasted little legs, and looked altogether so unpleasantly amorous that Tom was quite disgusted with the levity of his behaviour . . ." (185). The chair recounts his youthful romantic adventures, noting that women were always fond of him, but soon gets to the point of his conversation. He wants Tom to marry the widow because the tall man is an adventurer, who would sell all the furniture and abscond, leaving the old chair himself to waste away in some broker's shop, whereas he knows that Tom would never leave the inn while there was anything left to drink there. To aid Tom, therefore, the chair tells him of a letter that reveals Jinkins, the tall man, to be already married. The next morning, Tom cannot draw the chair into conversation, but does find the letter, and with it informs the widow of the true situation and eventually marries her himself. At the end of the story there is discussion among its immediate audience whether it was believed to be true, and the bagman says Tom himself declared it was.

The personification in this tale is literally acted out, though the discussion about its verity calls its truthfulness into question for Dickens's reader. Garrett Stewart some time ago called attention not only to Dickens's inclination to personification, but also to his self-consciousness about it. Stewart writes of Tom's story:

> In the sober light of day, "it must have been a remarkably ingenious and lively imagination, that could have discovered any resemblance between it and an old man." Dickens himself, of course, has just such an imagination, and the whole tale seems to have unrolled from a simple instance of his typical descriptive trick—the animation of lifeless objects. (*Dickens and the Trials* 41)

Stewart gives an instance of Dickens's self-consciousness about the animating power of his mind by citing a passage from "The Parlour Orator" ("Characters," *Sketches* 5). Praise for the narrator's oratorical abilities follows his speech, after which the company disbands, leaving him alone with his mind. What takes place is an unusual revelation:

> "If we had followed the established precedent in all such instances, we should have fallen into a fit of musing, without delay . . . and we should have gone dreaming on, until the pewter pot on the table, or the little beer-chiller on the fire, had started into life, and addressed to us a long story of days gone by. But, by some means or other, we were not in a romantic humour; and although we tried very hard to invest the furniture with vitality, it remained perfectly unmoved, obstinate, and sullen." (17)

Stewart notes that Dickens has failed in this effort because of the false rhetoric of another speaker; such false rhetoric is an enemy of romantic fancy.

In *Versions of Pygmalion*, J. Hillis Miller argues that all story telling is an act of prosopopoeia, "the ascription to entities that are not really alive first of a name, then of a face, and finally, in a return to language, of a voice" (5). The author and narrator create living characters out of nothing living, just as Pygmalion creates his statue of a woman, which takes on real life as Galatea. Miller argues that characters thus created take on a life of their own and thus escape the dominion of both author and narrator, for the reader also performs an act of prosopopoeia by giving life to mere markings on a page. Dickens seems to have intuited, in Tom Smart's case, the insight that Miller has worked out logically. He, as author, has created a narrator who brings Tom Smart to life, who in turn brings the chair to life. But Dickens also implies in this episode his own interest in retaining control of his begotten Galateas, for just as Tom makes use of the chair to achieve the fulfillment of his own desires, so the bagman achieves his purpose in conveying an amazing tale, which leaves him still in a position of narrative power. Though his audience are left doubting whether they have Pygmalion's power to make these characters real or to discount them as frauds, this abeyance, in turn, leaves Dickens, not the reader, in control of the interpolated tale and its context in the larger narrative.

And yet the bagman has told his tale with realistic detail and engaging humor that makes it a success as a story, with the one exception of the talking chair, which should place it outside the realm of realism. Personification is a literary device that does not sit well with realistic literature. Metaphors and similes can be recognized as tropes common to ordinary language, and often seen as necessary to clear communication, but personification serves no such utilitarian end, operating largely for its own effects.[2] In the bagman's tale the talking chair makes the truthfulness of the tale impossible as a realistic narrative. Thus, at the outset of his career, Dickens very clearly notes the antagonism between personification and realistic narrative, and chooses sides. He is not deeply interested in realism, despite the acclaim he received, and continues to receive, for the detailed realism of his writing. Rather, like Jack Bamber, who narrates a tale himself later in *Pickwick,* Dickens wishes to depict "'the romance of life, sir, the romance of life!'" (279).

In midcareer, Dickens made another memorable use of personification in a narrative that was clearly not intended to be realistic. I refer to *A Christmas Carol.* Scrooge returns to his chambers on Christmas Eve. "They were a gloomy suite of rooms, in a lowering pile of building up a yard, where it had so little business to be, that one could scarcely help fancying it must have run there when it was a young house, playing at hide-and-seek with other houses, and forgotten the way out again" (14). This personification is qualified by the fact that it is merely fancied, but it has particular point, since just before this description, we have been told that Bob Crachitt has hurried home to play at blindman's buff. The old house is long past play now, as is Scrooge, but in the overall atmosphere of the story, the house's fate seems to foretell the mood that would fall upon the Crachitts if Tiny Tim died. And the theme of death is immediately raised by a more startling personification, for Scrooge comes to his door and undergoes a shock.

> And then let any man explain to me, if he can, how it happened that Scrooge, having his key in the lock of the door, saw in the knocker, without its undergoing any intermediate process of change—not a knocker, but Marley's face. (15)

This might not be considered true personification, because the knocker does not have an identity of its own. Nonetheless, an inanimate object takes on human qualities—very specific human qualities. There is a further irony in this apparition, since it was customary in Victorian times to muffle door knockers when there was illness or death in a house; instead, Marley perversely appears alive again as a knocker. This irony highlights the conflict between personification and realism. Scrooge does not want to believe in the visions he experiences, and tells Marley's ghost when it appears: "'There's more of gravy than of grave about you, whatever you are!'" (18). He does not wish to believe in what is not realistic, yet he is forced to endure an experience that is well beyond the range of the real. Before he encountered the knocker, Scrooge was described as lacking any fancy, but, for Dickens, fancy—the capacity to use one's imagination—was essential to a satisfactory life.[3] Personification is a striking manifestation of a fanciful mind, and thus an endorsement for Dickens's preferred mode of narrating.

The episode with Marley and the knocker is adumbrated in the sketch "Our Next-Door Neighbour," in *Sketches by Boz*, which opens with the narrator's theory of door knockers. He asserts "that between the man and his knocker, there will inevitably be a greater or less degree of resemblance and sympathy" (40). A large round lion-faced knocker is invariably owned by a convivial fellow, but a small attorney or bill-broker will patronize a knocker lion with a "countenance expressive of savage stupidity"—it is "a great favourite with the selfish and brutal" (40). Little spare priggish men prefer "a little pert Egyptian knocker, with a long thin face, a pinched-up nose, and a very sharp chin" (40). This amusing identification of human character with door knockers is not personification, but it demonstrates Dickens's ready penchant for aligning the animate and the inanimate. It also makes explicit the function of passages like the one from *Pickwick* with which I began this chapter. Just as Pickwick's mood is extended to the animate and inanimate things around him, so men extend their characters to their doorknockers.

Various critics have called attention to certain tensions in Dickens's fiction that I believe are relevant here. Susan Horton notes the mechanical use of repetition in Dickens's fiction, while also indicating that Dickens greatly disliked what appeared mechanical (100ff). She draws the conclusion that: "Since sameness or stasis is the beginning of the death of feeling, the Victorians love its opposite: violent contrasts" (107). And Dickens satisfies that love by constantly shifting modes of presentation. John Kucich makes a related observation. "In effect, by absorbing machine-like language into his own narration, Dickens out-machines the machine, performing with the very impersonal linguistic energy he can at the same time condemn in his characters" (214).[4] For me, the tension between the repetitions either rhetorical or diegetic is of a piece with Dickens's dramatic vision of a world both perilous and safe, comprehensible and mysterious, good and evil. Susan Horton puts it differently, but tending in the same direction. She says that Dickens diverts the reader with an unending parade of miscellaneous human beings, but they remind us of exactly those things we most need to escape from (65). The consequence of this "struggle" in Dickens's fiction is ordinarily a happy ending, with even the ghosts that haunt characters helping them to a better comprehension of their place in the world. Hence Marley's face animating the knocker is prelude to an experience that will open a metaphorical doorway into an improved future for Scrooge. I believe that personification, the animation of inanimate objects, is related to this overall narrative drive.

On the borderline with actual personification is another form of identification with the inanimate closely related to the house owner and his door knocker. This is the interest in objects for their own sake. A very simple example of this approach also appears early in *Sketches by Boz* in "Shops and Their Tenants," where the narrator follows with personal interest, his "old friend," a certain building holding various shops in succession in its progress through decline to degradation. It is almost like following the moral decline of a fellow human, although the building is seen more as a victim than an agent of that decline. More intimate yet is the connection so acutely examined by J. Hillis Miller between clothing and its former owners in the sketch "Meditations in Monmouth Street," mentioned in a previous chapter, where the narrator imagines the kinds of people who wore the various items of clothing and even creates brief stories of their lives (Miller, *Sketches* 1ff). The articles of clothing themselves do not take on life, but recall what is metonymically associated with them. They are Galateas now once more returned to stone.

"Meditations in Monmouth Street" is a *tour de force* of creative reportage and meant to be perceived as such, but Dickens uses a similar technique in his fiction, sometimes to very complicated effect. Dickens was as much given to deanimating the human as he was to animating the nonhuman, a version of the contrast between mechanism and dynamism mentioned above. There are intriguing examples of this method in *Dombey and Son*. Dombey is a man unconcerned with the imagination and devoted to material things, especially those involved with commerce, especially money, so it is not surprising that when his son is born he anticipates passing on his wealth and his name to him. His daughter, Florence, however, he regards, because she is a girl, as "merely a piece of base coin . . ." (3). Dickens can, here and elsewhere in the novel, slyly reveal the mindsets of his characters through such deanimations (just as he can with their animations). But the narrator himself is already at work to prepare the reader for outcomes of the plot through his own anima-tions, particularly in his description of Dombey himself on the first page of the novel. "On the brow of Dombey, Time and his brother Care had set some marks, as on a tree that was to come down in good time—remorseless twins they are for striding through their human forests, notching as they go . . ." (1). Not only has Dombey been transformed into a tree, as though he were a figure out of Ovid's *Metamorphosis,* but the abstractions Time and Care have assumed human characters as though they were in an allegory such as *Pilgrim's Progress.* But even more significant is the proleptic hint that the upright tree is destined for a fall—something that is delayed until Dombey's ruin near the end of the novel. Elsewhere, Dombey is described as wooden or as a piece of statuary. At a dinner dreadful to others, "Mr. Dombey alone remained unmoved. He might have been hung up for sale at a Russian fair as a specimen of a frozen gentleman" (57). He may retain his human form, but the great merchant has been transformed into an inanimate being now an object for a commercial venture, not its organizer. Earlier in the novel Dombey is likened to money itself; he "was one of those close-shaved close-cut moneyed gentlemen who are glossy and crisp like new bank-notes, and who seem to be artificially braced and tightened as by the stimulating action of golden shower-baths" (17). Dombey's stiffness is associated not only with his concern for wealth, but also with his pride and egotism. Also greatly given to egotism is another unappealing character Major Bagstock, who is also "wooden-featured" (83).

If negative characters have their animation compromised by various tropes, a livelier figure in the novel is the nonhuman wooden midshipman, "which thrust itself out above the pavement, right leg foremost, with a sua-vity the least endurable," who represents the true domestic sanctuary of Sol Gill's shop (32). Hence, while humans are turned into wood, wood has conferred upon it pert but attractive qualities that suggest the kind of long-lasting fidelity and integrity manifested by both Sol and Captain Cuttle. This is clearly not accidental writing, but coding with a vengeance. At the same time, the wooden midshipman can mimic the traits of humans. Both Dombey and Bagstock are depicted as relatively heartless men, and the wooden midshipman can behave as they do.

The Wooden Midshipman at the Instrument-maker's door, like the hard-hearted little midshipman he was, remained supremely indifferent to Wal-ter's going away, even when the very last day of his sojourn in the back parlour was on the decline. With his quadrant at his round black knob of an eye, and his figure in its old attitude of indomitable alacrity, the midship-man displayed his elfin small clothes to the best advantage, and, absorbed in scientific pursuits, had no sympathy with worldly concerns. (258)

Of course, a wooden midshipman may be forgiven for remaining heartless, since he truly is made of wood, but he stands out as an indictment against the unfeeling men in the novel who have pulsing hearts, but do not heed them. Dickens thus uses animation in a way prohibited to realism, for it works toward the intensifying of his novel's scheme, and emphasizes its fanciful over its factual elements.

More striking yet in the way of deanimating humans and animating the nonliving is *Hard Times,* the opening of which offers a sophisticated example of dehumanization and personification engaged in a hand-to-hand struggle. Thomas Gradgrind has been speaking about the necessity for facts.

> The emphasis was helped by the speaker's square wall of a forehead, which had his eyebrows for its base, while his eyes found commodious cellarage in two dark caves, overshadowed by the wall. The emphasis was helped by the speaker's mouth, which was wide, thin, and hard set. The emphasis was helped by the speaker's voice, which was inflexible, dry, and dictatorial. The emphasis was helped by the speaker's hair, which bristled on the skirts of his bald head, a plantation of firs to keep the wind from its shining surface, all covered with knobs, like the crust of a plum pie, as if the head had scarcely warehouse-room for the hard facts stored inside. The speaker's obstinate carriage, square coat, square legs, square shoulders—nay, his very neckcloth, trained to take him by the throat with an unaccommodating grasp, like a stubborn fact, as it was—all helped the emphasis. (7)

Here is an apt way to open a novel whose theme is the conflict of Fact (or Realism) and Fancy. The spokesman for fact has his human qualities obscured. His forehead is a wall overshadowing a cellarage. His sparse hair is a line of trees to protect the bald surface of his head, which itself is knobbed with projections like those on the crust of a plum pie. All of these images dehumanize Gradgrind, but they are energetically at war with one another as well, for the softness of the crust of the pie seems to belie the stoniness of the forehead. However, this is just one sly way of indicating that the rigidity of belief in facts has a similar fault. The facts stored in the warehouse of Gradgrind's mind are pushing through the pulpy surface of his head. The mind is better served by containing some airier ballast of fancy. And facts themselves seem to know this better than the philosophers who promote their hegemony, for, in the personification of the neckcloth, they take the living man by the throat as though to strangle him and deprive him of life— the ultimate dehumanization.

The narrator anticipates the negative characters themselves by appropriating their inhuman perspective and applying it to them just before he discloses what their outlook is. The three fact-worshipping men in this scene "swept with their eyes the inclined plane of little vessels then and there arranged in order, ready to have imperial gallons of facts poured into them until they were full to the brim" (7–8). These men feel that walls decorated with horses or carpets with flowers are unacceptable because they violate the principle of realism. It is clear from the outset of *Hard Times,* that Dickens will himself engage in a battle against such realism by using the tools of fairy tale, exotic narratives, and other resources of fancy, as he makes clear with his apostrophe to Mr. M'Choakumchild, himself, like other schoolmasters, "lately turned at the same time, in the same factory, on the same principles, like so many pianoforte legs" (12).

> He went to work, in this preparatory lesson, not unlike Morgiana in the Forty Thieves: looking into all the vessels ranged before him, one after another, to see what they contained. Say, good M'Choakumchild. When from thy boiling store thou shalt fill each jar brimful by-and-by, dost thou think that thou wilt always kill outright the robber Fancy lurking within—or sometimes only maim him and distort him? (12)

Here Dickens turns the tables on the fact men. While they perceived the children merely as vessels, Dickens now appropriates those vessels and puts the living if maimed spirit of Fancy back into them, using as his medium *The Arabian Nights,* a text the adults would abominate as nothing but Fancy.

If disagreeable humans are thus deanimated, the unappealing city of Coketown is contrarily given life. Its walls are "red and black like the painted face of a savage," and from its tall chimneys come "interminable serpents of smoke," while the pistons of the steam engine work up and down "like the head of an elephant in a state of melancholy madness" (22). If these unliving things are brought to life, it is not a promising life, but a foreign and threatening place, suggestive of an Indian tropical forest. The negative effect of Coketown and its owners (the fact men) is made manifest at the end of the novel when Tom Gradgrind appears with a painted face to help effect his escape from the law in a foreign country where he dies of a fever. This could be the West Indies, India, or any other part of the British empire, but the early ominous description of Coketown forecasts and hovers over young Tom's fate.

Two instances of the inanimate world taking on human powers in a minatory way occur in *Bleak House.* One is the third-person narrator's warning that the slum Tom-All-Alone will have its revenge on those who have occasioned its neglect. The other is the clock that speaks out, telling the doomed Tulkinghorn "Don't go home." Both instances clearly violate the spirit of realism and do so self-consciously. Dickens wants his readers to think of the natural and the man-made world as having a meaning that is discoverable by the imagination, not merely by reason and the interpretation of facts. Virgil Grillo remarks that "Dickens' novels offer us a world where character and object merge; where symbolic identifications are more than comments on human personality; character and symbol merge in an almost totemic system" (211). Metonymy, such a valuable tool for the realists, here becomes not merely identification of a character with some object, but a merging with it, an assumption of its nonhuman traits.[5] But the opposite is also true, as human traits are transferred to objects. Mildred Newcome argues that Dickens's mode of experience can be visualized as a figured tapestry or pictorial scroll interpreting life, containing allegorical people, emblematic places, and so forth (2ff). She contends that internal and external realities blend in the interpretation of experience. For her, Dickens knows that he is reweaving parts or all of the total allegory of the pilgrimage of life (189). I agree that Dickens's narratives share certain qualities with allegory, though they never become precisely that. Nonetheless, his bestowing on humans traits associated with inanimate life and his personification of the inanimate, resemble that feature of allegory that makes humans and objects manifestations of moral traits. In *The Pilgrim's Progress,* which Dickens knew and loved, a wicket is not merely a wicket, but a gateway into a new life. A broom is not merely a broom, but an instrument of human imagination.

I want to end and summarize with a few brief examples from *The Uncommercial Traveller* that illustrate Dickens's tendency to exchange human and nonhuman traits in a way that works against a simple realist practice. I choose *The Uncommercial Traveller* as a source because these essays, like the *Sketches by Boz* can easily be taken as realistic reportage, though I believe there is a hint at the romantic side of everyday things in the "Uncommercial" part of the title. The title of the essay "Shy Neighborhoods" already suggests a transfer of human qualities to nonhuman space. It turns out largely to be a study of animals. The narrator calls attention to the bad company birds keep and makes similar comments on donkeys and dogs. Cats, he observes, tend toward barbarism in shy neighborhoods. But what interests me most in this essay is the narrator's observation that there are certain dogs who keep people. This reversal of the "natural" order is conspicuous. Dickens self-consciously shocks his readers out of the normal expectation that animals will be "kept" by humans. It is a conscious part of Dickens's literary arsenal.

In "The City of the Absent" the Uncommercial Traveller meditates on all of the empty locations, such as banks, that people do not go to on Sunday as though they were acquaintances neglected, while in "Arcadian London," which also deals with a London emptied of many of its citizens in August, the narrator muses on the grim dentist's room that is now doing penance. These places are treated as humanlike not because they metonymically suggest their human counterparts; they are humanized precisely because no humans are there to compete with them. It is the absence of humans that calls up in the narrator's imagination the possible humanity of nonhuman entities.

Finally, in "Aboard Ship," generally a very straightforward account of the narrator's experiences on a ship crossing the Atlantic from New York to Liverpool, one passage sharply calls attention to itself and shifts the moral register of the whole piece. Early in the essay the narrator recalls odd church services that once were practiced aboard ship. A little later he argues that, despite temperance opponents, there is no harm in the distribution of grog to sailors. These references to issues that fall within the realm of morality take on a different cast when the narrator describes the constant noise of the screw propeller as like the voice of conscience, always there. Soon after, as though prompted by a bad conscience himself, he ponders the many dangers of sea travel. Turning the inanimate propeller into a moral guide is precisely the kind of trick Dickens often uses to defamiliarize his material for his readers and make them take notice. What is a little taking of grog in the large scale of moral behavior when your life itself might be in the balance? If our conscience must always be working, let it work on serious matters.

Some time ago, J. Hillis Miller wrote a brilliant study of *Sketches by Boz.* I have already referred to his treatment of "Meditations in Monmouth Street." Elsewhere I differ with Miller concerning Dickens's use of metonymy, but I agree with the following passage.

> If a movement from things to people to stories is the habitual structural principle of the *Sketches,* the law which validates this movement is the assumption of a necessary similarity between a man, his environment, and the life he is forced to lead within that environment. (14)

What I have argued in this chapter is that Dickens was fully aware of his own perception of the relationship of persons to places and things, and one way for him to make his readers aware of this relationship as well was to exchange human and nonhuman, animate and inanimate traits within his narratives. So humans lose some of their humanity and become wooden like trees, or dark and forbidding like caves, while chairs and buildings take on the ability to speak or to become ill and infirm. Some of the most interesting instances of this practice are points of amalgamation, such as the wooden advertising sign in the form of a midshipman—where the wood has a human form and is credited with human behavioral traits—or Marley's face that appears as a door knocker. In these instances, the genuinely human and the genuinely nonhuman merge, with the balance toward the latter in the midshipman and toward the former with Marley. But in both instances, and as a regular aspect of his writing, Dickens was trying to demonstrate his narrative control over his readers by exceeding the self-imposed limits of literary realism, and employing techniques related to emotions deeply embedded in the human imagination. He did not want to be a mere realist, master though he was of many of its techniques. He wanted rather to be something closer to a magus.

CHAPTER 6

The Riches of Redundancy

Our Mutual Friend

O ur *Mutual Friend* has not pleased many otherwise satisfied readers of Dickens's fiction. For his contemporaries and such acute assessors of fiction as Henry James, the novel seemed to lack structure, among other faults.[1] More recently, critics have discovered ways in which Dickens can be seen experimenting in this novel, especially with a tightness of structure that, to a large extent, keeps itself hidden.[2] What I wish to argue here is that Dickens was in full command of his narrative, so much so that he wanted both to assist his readers in interpreting it correctly and to retain control of the mode of that interpretation, impulses that go against the ambitions of realism. Dickens was a man devoted to orderliness and careful exertion to a determined end. These inclinations, it seems to me, are extended to his fiction as well, more so as he grows older. I also wish to argue that in establishing an incredibly elaborate structure for his novel, he was extending his quarrel with what has come to be known as realism. Calling attention to its own language and using highly formal structure were taboos of realism.[3] Dickens glories in his command of language, especially metaphor, and creates a formal structure that intentionally challenges plausibility. In *Our Mutual Friend,* Dickens employs his characteristic technique of offering a surplus of information in order to guarantee the transmission of meaning, what in information theory was early dubbed "redundancy."[4] In his early fiction, Dickens was rather obvious about this overload of data—the backing up of one pattern of references by another related pattern. But by the time he wrote *Our Mutual Friend*, his technique, though still perceivable, was subtler, hence my choice of this novel to study redundancy because it weaves imagery, allusion, and narrative detail into a mode of transmission that calls attention to itself and by doing so restricts what the information it transmits can mean. Insofar as it does this, it is directly opposed to the practices of realist fiction. In his early fiction, Dickens was serializing narratives of which he did not know the conclusions and his use of imagery was thus not as controlled as it became later. For this reason, the early novels are in some ways closer to realist technique than the later, though with a powerful admixture of fairy-tale qualities. There are many more examples of the gratuitous details that constitute Roland Barthes's "reality effect," undigested material that emphasizes the unexpectedness of everyday reality. In the later, well-planned novels, Dickens permitted very little that did not contribute to his design; the superfluity of information both in narrated detail and in the supporting imagery and allusiveness, despite immediate appearances, acts against this "reality effect," by narrowing the meaning of the narrative as a whole and confining it as strictly as possible to Dickens's own intended meaning. Like his own characters Jenny Wren and Mr. Venus, he wants to make use of every scrap. Even the serial mode of publication came to serve these ends as the segments became more tightly related to one another, as book and chapter titles often indicate; see, for example, the allusive book titles of *Our Mutual Friend* itself. Yet if the technique in the late fiction was subtler, so were Dickens's signals to his readership on how to read his texts. The opening of the novel is Dickens's primer on the reading of signs, aptly titled "On the Look-out."

The first chapter opens with a description of Gaffer and Lizzie Hexam in a boat on the Thames and begins with a series of exclusions. Gaffer has "no net, no hook, or line, and he could not be a fisherman"; other items not present are listed and the trades of waterman and lighterman are eliminated as possible occupations. In fact, "there is no clue to what [Gaffer] looked for, but he looked for something, with a most intent and searching gaze."[5] The passage alerts us to the fact that we too will need "clues" to solve the mystery of this boat and its occupants, who are obviously "doing something they often did, and were seeking what they often sought" (1). The scene is filled with the need to interpret. Lizzie must read Gaffer's face to direct the boat she is rowing, just as Gaffer reads the water for signs of what he is seeking. But while Gaffer's gaze is utilitarian, Lizzie's is affected by emotion and fancy. A slant of light upon "a rotten stain [at the bottom of the boat] which bore some resemblance to the outline of a muffled human form, coloured it as though with diluted blood. This caught the girl's eye, and she shivered" (2). This is one of the narrator's many clues to his readers in this short opening chapter; it emphasizes Lizzie's figural imagination. But another clue is the narrator's own figure. Gaffer is likened to "a roused bird of prey" (3), an image confirmed by Rogue Riderhood, who says to Gaffer, "'you're like the wulturs, pardner, and scent 'em out'" (4). Though the mystery of what Gaffer scents out and what Lizzie cannot bear to sit close to is undisclosed, a transparent clue appears at the very close of the chapter, when we learn that a neophyte might fancy "that the ripples passing over it [what Gaffer has in tow] were dreadfully like faint changes of expression on a sightless face; but Gaffer was no neophyte and had no fancies" (5).

In this first chapter, then, the narrator gives us a lesson in reading signs and establishes the basis for some of the central themes of the narrative—preying and scavenging, the transformative powers of water, and the contrast of fancy with pragmatic thought, all of these interwoven with one another from the start. Another theme is begun, but left unpursued in the description of Gaffer's boat being "[a]llied to the bottom of the river rather than the surface, by reason of the slime and ooze with which it was covered . . ." (1). But if the narrator has given us a lesson in reading signs, he has not openly solved the mystery of the chapter. Who are Gaffer, Lizzie, and Rogue? What is their business? What does Gaffer have in tow? If we have learned our lesson and read the clues, we should know.

Chapter 2 abandons the river for a very different setting where the subject and theme of dust is prominent in the tale of old John Harmon, a narrative that interests the company gathered at the Veneerings' home. In telling the story of the Harmons, Mortimer Lightwood remarks that old Harmon's daughter "intimated that she was secretly engaged to that popular character whom the novelists and versifiers call Another," and a bit later declares that "[w]e must now return, as the novelists say, and as we all wish they wouldn't, to the man from Somewhere" (14). As central story teller in chapter 2, Lightwood alludes directly and critically, even condescendingly, to conventions of fiction; appropriately, his own narrative is incomplete and ends abruptly until a message suddenly delivered to him provides closure to the story of the man from Somewhere. His listeners speculate, one notion being that there was a codicil in the dust, but all the auditors are wrong. Lightwood exclaims, "[t]he story is completer and rather more exciting than I supposed. Man's drowned!" (17).[6]

Chapters 1 and 2 could not be much more different from one another—the one set in the ooze and damp of the river with ghastly circumstances developing, the other set among the well-to-do and cultivated classes enjoying a stagy dinner, with the luxury of speculating on the life stories of strangers concerned with dust and money. Chapter 1 is narrated by an alert narrator; chapter 2 is *about* narration. But dust and water come together at the end of chapter 2 in the supposed drowning death of John Harmon, Jr. When dust and water mingle, the result is mud and ooze, and as the narrative progresses we discover how significant mud is in the meaning of the story, if we have learned to read the clues the way Dickens has taught us to do. But for us to read these clues correctly, we must have a surplus of them. *Our Mutual Friend* offers an ideal example of how Dickens utilizes redundancy not merely to reinforce narrative meaning, but to assert his control of how that meaning will be received, and also to indicate the limitations of the realist program. Patterns of imagery, recurrent motifs, and repetitions of themes are common in many types of fiction, but Dickens subsumes all of these and the narrative design of the novel itself to a mode of transmission that makes each of these devices reinforce the others, thereby more severely circumscribing the meaning of the information it conveys even as it becomes denser. Redundancy can be seen as a mode of interpretation something like the concept of the implied author, where an idealized governing force of the narrative is posited for much of the narrative's design. Redundancy can be seen as such a governing force imbedded in the novel's language itself, but requiring both by its intricacy and its self-advertizing a specific mode of information reception. In some ways, it is a mode of meaning that is the opposite of Bakhtin's heteroglossia.

Redundancy means different things in different contexts, though ordinarily it suggests superfluousness. The Victorians, for example, discussed the problem of redundant women, a large surplus of single women for whom there were insufficient mates. Different fields of research today use the concept of redundancy in a rigorous manner. In linguistics and semiotics it has to do with that which is supposedly unnecessary though helpful for the communication of information (though often such redundancy is difficult to determine). W. C. Watt notes that "the kinds of information that are 'redundant' (superfluous, predictable) vary greatly depending on what task is at hand"; his example is the recognition of letters of the alphabet (16).

> Suppose some performative differences, in so far as they depend on utilizing different portions of one's overall knowledge of the letters, might be reflected *directly* in the letters' analysis in a particularly simple way: information used in some tasks but not in others could be included in the letters' analysis, at some level, as "redundant." (17)

What is redundant depends upon what task is required; for example, recognizing, uttering, or writing a letter of the alphabet.

Although such concepts of redundancy are obviously related to that which I am using here, my derivation is more directly from information theory.[7] Here is Jeremy Campbell's explanation.

> In nearly all forms of communication, more messages are sent than are strictly necessary to convey the information intended by the sender. Such additional messages diminish the unexpectedness, the surprise effect, of the information itself, making it more predictable. This extra ration of predictability is called redundancy, and it is one of the most important concepts in information theory. Redundancy is essentially a constraint. It limits the value of W in the entropy equation $S = k \log W$, reducing the number of ways in which the various parts of a system can be arranged. (68)[8]

Language is an example where redundancy is contained within rules. In order to communicate in language there must be shared conventions such as grammar, spelling, and so forth. Attempts to compress language, deleting what appears to be redundant, destroy the built-in safeguards against error found in all languages. Redundancy in this sense facilitates the communication of messages. Campbell continues, "[t]here is yet another aspect of redundancy which is of great interest. This is the role it plays in enabling systems, both biological organisms and artificial intelligence machines, to become complex. . . . The more complex the system the more likely it is that one of its parts will malfunction. Redundancy is a means of keeping the system running in the presence of malfunction" (73). Campbell concludes that "while redundancy constrains, it also may lead to great complexity within the constraints" (74).

Redundancy might apply in any number of situations. Campbell cites Susumu Ohno, a geneticist who speculated that evolution provided "'useless information' in the DNA of organisms. This came in the form of repetition, which is the simplest form of redundancy . . ." (149). But this "useless information" can prove to be very useful indeed, as Jennifer Ackerman indicates in her account of heredity.

> But lately scientists have taken a closer look at the wilderness of junk DNA and found that certain stretches are fecund voids, like Leonardo's darks, full of sequences that may be ungenelike but are nevertheless vital to life, exerting exquisite control over the genes embedded in them. (24)

Any code, any message, could contain within it a useless or a useful redundancy, but the implications of biology, linguistics, information theory, and other areas of study suggest that wherever redundancy exists, it contributes to the delivery of a message.[9] Lily E. Kay provides an interesting account of how the concept of redundancy crossed the borders from linguistics to genetics and back again by way of a conference of the American Academy of Arts and Sciences in Boston, August, 1962 (304ff).[10] The codes of genetics and linguistics might be different, but the concept of redundancy as a principle of communication need not be.

I am not suggesting that Dickens understood this notion, but simply that he intuitively comprehended the way in which a message can be delivered by a combination of constraint and increasing complexity through narrative language. *Bleak House* provides a midcareer sample. That novel is famous for the repetitions of its opening paragraphs, tolling the words 'mud' and 'fog' over and over. But that is an obvious example of repetition, a transparent descriptive redundancy. A less prominent pattern also begins with the first chapter and continues throughout the novel until it swells to major significance in the death of Lady Dedlock. Chapter 1 ends with this memorable sentence: "If all the injustice [Chancery] has committed, and all the misery it has caused, could only be locked up with it, and the whole burnt away in a great funeral pyre,—why so much the better for other parties than the parties in Jarndyce and Jarndyce" (7). And so much the better for all of English society, the passage and the chapter suggest. The end of a chapter is a good place to locate an important theme, and Dickens does that here by introducing the funeral/burial motif. But it is not only the world of Chancery that would be better off in its grave. The world of fashion represented in chapter 2 by the Dedlock household at Chesney Wold seems already to have passed the boundary between the quick and the dead at least metaphorically, but literally as well. Chesney Wold seems inclined in that direction. The little church in the park is moldy, "and there is a general smell and taste of the ancient Dedlocks in their graves" (9). When Esther first visits the locale, she notices that the church "smelt as earthy as the grave" (249). It is at this moment that Esther first sees Lady Dedlock, who will later learn that Esther is her own daughter returned from the grave. Tom Lloyd has commented on some of the connections between Lady Dedlock and Esther, including the irony that the mother must "bury" her newly discovered daughter in secrecy again, but also that the handkerchief that Esther uses to cover Jenny's dead baby in a respectful funeral rite, is later taken by Lady Dedlock in her ultimately fatal flight.[11] So the handkerchief becomes a signifier in the funerary connection between Esther and Lady Dedlock. Jo, too, makes a connection between Esther and the woman who wanted him to show her the "berryin' ground" (430). These, and many other similar references, create by their repetition a redundant network alluding to funerals and burials, including the elaborate inquest sequence following the death of Nemo, that peaks in the scene in which Esther discovers her mother dead at the gates of the loathsome burying ground where her one-time lover and the father of Esther is buried. By the end of the novel, we realize that these redundancies have pointed the way to the conclusion, with Lady Dedlock in her grave.

> It is known for certain that the handsome Lady Dedlock lies in the mauso-leum in the park, where the trees arch darkly overhead, and the owl is heard at night making the woods ring; but whence she was brought home, to be laid among the echoes of that solitary place, or how she died, is all mystery. Some of her old friends, principally to be found among the peachy-cheeked charmers with the skeleton throats, did once occasionally say, as they toyed in a ghastly manner with large fans—like charmers reduced to flirting with grim Death, after losing all their other beaux—did once occasionally say, when the World assembled together, that they wondered the ashes of the Dedlocks, entombed in the mausoleum, never rose against the profanation of her company. But the dead-and-gone Dedlocks take it very calmly, and have never been known to object. (872)

This scene of the nearly dead judging the dead is reinforced by the implica-tion that the entire Dedlock way of life is passing away, supplanted implic-itly by the inhabitants of new Bleak House, a place of joy and healing. Sir Leicester is the manifestation of this impending change.

> Closed in by night with broad screens, and illumined only in that part, the light of the drawing-room seems gradually contracting and dwindling until it shall be no more. A little more, in truth, and it will be all extinguished for Sir Leicester; and the damp door in the mausoleum which shuts so tight, and looks so obdurate, will have opened and received him. (874)

The anonymous narrator concludes that "passion and pride . . . have died away from the place in Lincolnshire . . ." (876).[12] And so the penultimate chapter ends, but in the final chapter, narrated by Esther, the turf has not yet been planted on Richard Carstone's grave when his son is born, symbolizing a new era of new hopes when even Esther's lost looks can come to life again.

This brief taste of Dickens's method of providing a superfluity of informa-tion on a theme he wishes to convey is one manifestation of what is more densely enacted in *Our Mutual Friend*. Literal and metaphorical funerary and burial activity abound in *Bleak House,* but the mesh of references to water, dust, and mud is far more complex in *Our Mutual Friend*. We have already seen how the themes of water, dust, surface, and depth are devel-oped in the first two chapters of this novel, but we have scarcely, as it were, touched the surface. The whole second chapter depends upon the concept of the Veneerings as representative of superficiality, as their name suggests. But set against this reprehensible surfaceness is the desire to penetrate surfaces, and we get a glimpse of this immediately at the beginning of chapter 3, when Mortimer interrogates Charley Hexam, who has written and delivered the note about John Harmon's death. This interrogation takes place in the Veneering library with its "bran-new books, in bran-new bindings . . ." (18). Young Charley "glanced at the backs of the books, with an awakened curiosity that went below the binding," notes the narrator, then adds, "[n]o one who can read, ever looks at a book, even unopened on a shelf, like one who cannot," a telling connection of the surface/depth theme with that of interpreting signs and that of narration.

Charley takes Mortimer to Gaffer, who is vain about not being able to read, yet being "scholar enough" to identify all of the posters on the walls of his room, which refer to corpses he has recovered (22). This mesh of themes is drawn together more forcefully, though the reader does not know it at this point, when the man from Somewhere shows up at Gaffer's door seeking directions to the corpse, which he thinks he might be able to identify. Before chapter 3 ends, we meet another interpreter of signs in Lizzie Hexam, who can read the flames in the fireplace. Unlike Gaffer's ability to note the meaning of outside signs through his memory of what they stand for, Lizzie projects her own depths unto the unmeaning "signs" of the flames. Hence, all three Hexams are readers, but they span a very wide range of that activity; Lizzie's "reading" comes closest of the three to the related practice of narrating.

Having stated his themes and interwoven them in the opening three chapters, the narrator is now able to begin the more leisurely development of his story, and so the next two chapters introduce new key players in the novel, first the Wilfers and then Wegg and the Boffins. But gradually one or another theme is reintroduced. Boffin hires Wegg to read to him, though what is being read now becomes relatively inconsequential. However, what is important is that, whether or not he is a good reader, Wegg is an untrustworthy narrator. He has made up his account of the family in the corner house near which he has his stand. He is only one breeder of fictions, though, as the novel demonstrates. Chapter 10, for example, shows how Twemlow recognizes that "the Veneering guests become infected with the Veneering fiction," without realizing that he is infected too (115).

The first few chapters of *Our Mutual Friend* put Dickens's machinery in place. These are the cocoons of the redundancy to be spun out later. But having got this material before the reader, he relaxes into the "realistic" body of narrative. Still, the themes of the opening appear in trace amounts throughout, often linked to one of the other motives. Dickens was intent on keeping control of his own narrative and so, along with guiding his readers' interpretations, he includes examples of the misinterpretation of signs. Mr. Podsnap thinks that he knows what all signs mean, though the narrator checks his confidence abruptly when the foreign gentleman misunderstands Podsnap's boasting of the signs of prosperity in London, taking him to be referring to the horse dung so common on the London streets. This passage may seem gratuitous except that dung in the streets may reasonably be connected to the activities of a prosperous city. No business and wealth, no horses and their waste. But dung is also collected by scavengers and deposited in mounds that can also produce wealth, as they did for John Harmon, Sr. If Podsnap is thus negatively connected to the elder Harmon, he is also connected to the younger Harmon, for it is Podsnap who bids Veneering, "who has prospered exceedingly on the Harmon Murder," to retell the story. As Mr. Veneering plunges into the case, his wife dives into the same waters for a wealthy Ship-Broker as audience and brings him up, "safe and sound, by the hair" (134). This is a gruesomely comic reversal of what has supposedly happened to John Harmon, who is supposed not to have been brought up safe and sound.

This multipurpose imagery, what Garrett Stewart in a discussion of *Oliver Twist* calls "metaphoric overkill," (*The Cambridge Companion* 157) appears far too often for me to cite all cases in *Our Mutual Friend*. But Robert Alter admirably shows how what appears to be an isolated description of a foggy London reveals itself as thematically embedded, for the city drowning in fog with St. Paul's Cathedral the last to go, "carries forward the images of death by drowning" (136). Clearly Dickens's frequent and prominent references back to his initial themes are meant to keep the reader in training, but also to demonstrate his own command of the narrative. We are told of the "depths and shallows of Podsnappery" (255) and of the "winds and waves" of Fledgeby's stormy childhood (268). Betty Higden says she will be able to avoid the workhouse if there is "water enough to cover us" in England (327). Bradley Headstone's thoughts are "tributary" to one purpose (551). In the passage about Headstone, Dickens even provides a proleptic glimpse of the scene where Headstone will attack Wrayburn, so that, in rereading, his audience would recognize a sign missed in the initial reading.

These references to water are timid by comparison with more forceful passages in which water is connected with passionate, selfish, and even savage qualities. This connection is first made overtly at the very end of Book One in the chapter entitled "A Dismal Swamp," in which we learn of all of those who are trying to get money out of Boffin, who are described as "the Alligators of the Dismal Swamp, and are always lying by to drag the Golden Dustman under" (213). The chapter ends with a reference to Wegg as a "fish of the shark tribe in the Bower waters" who also resembles "some extinct bird," plotting to get his portion out of Boffin (213). This association is intensified when Boffin visits Venus's shop and has to hide behind a stuffed alligator upon Wegg's unexpected appearance to discuss the nefarious "friendly move" with Venus. The narrator remarks that Wegg's wicked behavior is nothing new. "The yard or two of smile on the part of the alligator might have been invested with the meaning, 'All about this was quite familiar knowledge down in the depths of the slime, ages ago'" (383). Wegg is connected to the slime in another way, for he resembles Gaffer as a bird of prey. He "fluttered over his prey," Boffin, even when he was powerless, but now, when he believes he has Boffin in his power, he prepares to "drop down upon" him (579, 584ff.).

Wegg's craving for Boffin's wealth is a hollow desire for gratification. A fiercer desire discloses itself in Bradley Headstone. He has advanced himself from humble origins of which he is both sullenly proud and ashamed. He employs a constant self-suppression in order to get on with his career as a schoolmaster. "Yet there was enough of what was animal, and of what was fiery (though smouldering), still visible in him, to suggest that if young Bradley Headstone, when a pauper lad, had chanced to be told off for the sea, he would not have been the last man in a ship's crew" (218). John Harmon recognizes something suppressed in Headstone. "The Secretary thought, as he glanced at the schoolmaster's face, that he had opened a channel here indeed, and that it was an unexpectedly dark and deep and stormy one, and difficult to sound" (388). But if Harmon cannot sound it, Headstone himself can, as he demonstrates to Lizzie, when he reveals his passion for her.

> "No man knows till the time comes what depths are within him. To some men it never comes; let them rest and be thankful! To me, you brought it; on me, you forced it; and the bottom of this raging sea," striking himself upon the breast, "has been heaved up ever since." (396)

The narrator can take a larger view of Headstone's individual case, and he does so in the same scene where he refers to Headstone's origins. "But even among school-buildings, school-teachers, and school-pupils, all according to pattern and all engendered in the light of the latest Gospel according to Monotony, the older pattern into which so many fortunes have been shaped for good and evil, comes out" (218). The narrator is referring to Miss Peecher, who has an unrequited passion for Headstone, but the passage applies equally to Headstone. The "older pattern" is what the alligator knows was commonplace in the slime ages ago. The slime and mire and mud are what humanity sinks to at its worst; it is what those who aspire to the best wish to rise out of. But there may be parodic versions of that ascent. Just as Headstone has risen above his origins, Charley Hexam wants to raise himself in the world and tells Lizzie "that after I have climbed up out of the mire, you shall not pull me down" (401, 403). Later, suspecting Headstone of criminal behavior, he disassociates himself from his former schoolmaster, saying "he will not be dragged down by others" (712–13). The playful "hunting" scenes that Wrayburn puts Headstone through on an almost nightly basis, making him "like an ill-timed wild animal," becomes a real hunting down of Wrayburn by Headstone (546). Ooze, slime, mud, and mire are the primordial savage conditions out of which the human race has presumably crept.

If the river bottom and the oozy river itself scavenged by birds of prey represent human vileness, it is a world supposedly best avoided and forgotten. And so, John Harmon, who has descended briefly into it, decides that John Harmon shall not come back to life; instead he buries "John Harmon many additional fathoms deep" (378). Like Headstone, Harmon as Rokesmith is determined to keep himself down, but in his case self-repression involves a consideration for others rather than a need for self-discipline.

All of the water references return near the end of the book as Wrayburn, having pursued Lizzie up the river, is attacked by Headstone then rescued by Lizzie.[13] Whereas Gaffer pulled the dead from the water to plunder them, Lizzie pulls Wrayburn from the water to save his life. All that she learned about her father's trade now serves to reverse it. The narrator cannot help reminding us of our reading lesson in the first chapter of the book, and notes that "An untrained sight would never have seen by the moonlight what she saw at the length of a few strokes astern" (700). It is still necessary to interpret signs correctly, to act rightly, just as Riderhood must decipher the meaning of Headstone's clothing (to implicate him in the murder) and then teach a lesson of his own in Headstone's own classroom. Rogue asks Headstone's students to name the waters on the earth, which they dutifully accomplish, but when he asks them what is caught in seas, rivers, lakes, and ponds, he has to correct the answers fish and weeds, and state that "It's suits o' clothes," for he has fished up the clothes that Headstone wore during the attack on Wrayburn (795). He is not now fishing up corpses, but empty suits of clothes, yet the parallel with the opening scenes of the novel is clear. In fact, Headstone is as good as a dead man already, as the erasure of his name from the blackboard portends, and he and Riderhood will soon end up together "lying under the ooze and scum" of the lock, back in the primordially savage world of which one was an obvious, the other a covert denizen (802).

As Wrayburn lies half-dead he fades in and out of consciousness, and the narrator remarks, "This frequent rising of a drowning man from the deep, to sink again, was dreadful to the beholders" (740). It is "the wreck of him that lay cast ashore there now . . ." (753). Having visited the river-side only through Lightwood's legal interest there, Wrayburn is attracted to Lizzie, who represents the positive element that can arise from the apparent unattractiveness of that world. It is she more than Charley who rises out of the mire and who lifts Wrayburn with her. And if he is a wrecked ship at this stage, he will survive to lead a better life married to Lizzie, who is, as Twemlow insists against the Voice of Society, a lady. If Lizzie is thus redemp-tive for Wrayburn, Harmon is similarly redemptive for Bella. Bella dreams of a rich husband coming to her in a ship and of setting off into the world as a wealthy woman (318ff), but later, after she has married Rokesmith, she says to her father that there was no John in all of the ships she had earlier imagined (670). In fact, there was. For John Harmon had returned in a ship from abroad specifically to investigate the circumstances that would have bound him to Bella as she was, not as she has become. Moreover, the result of their marriage is that a baby is on a ship coming to them, a baby that is safely brought home (688, 755), as John almost was not. The whole theme of water constitutes an extensive redundancy, but what seems superfluous is actually an elaborate network uniting various characters' histories, and various other themes. Water references, whether factual or metaphorical tell the complicated story of journeys on a perilous medium where some sink to the vile bottom and others land safely.

Lest we miss the larger meaning of the water motif, the narrator occa-sionally steps in to make it explicit. When Betty Higden is in flight from the workhouse she follows the Thames.

> In those pleasant little towns on Thames, you may hear the fall of the water over the weirs, or even, in still weather, the rustle of the rushes; and from the bridge you may see the young river, dimpled like a young child, playfully gliding away among the trees, unpolluted by the defilements that lie in wait for it on its course, and as yet out of hearing of the deep summons of the sea. It were too much to pretend that Betty Higden made out such thoughts; no; but she heard the tender river whispering to many like herself, 'Come to me, come to me! When the cruel shame and terror you have so long fled from, most beset you, come to me! I am the Relieving Officer appointed by eternal ordinance to do my work; I am not held in estimation according as I shirk it. My breast is softer than the pauper-nurse's; death in my arms is peacefuller than among the pauper-wards. Come to me!' (504–5)

Here is the opposite setting to the Dismal Swamp and the ancient slime. It is human innocence and human destiny. Betty Higden will soon die, but not in the river. Nor will Wrayburn die in the river. But the train carrying Mr.

Milvey to marry Wrayburn and Lizzie seems to suggest otherwise and certainly puts the water theme in a larger perspective as it roars across the river:

> spurning the watery turnings and doublings with ineffable contempt, and going straight to its end, as Father Time goes to his. To whom it is no matter what living waters run high or low, reflect the heavenly lights and darknesses, produce their little growth of weeds and flowers, turn here, turn there, are noisy or still, are troubled or at rest, for their course has one sure termination, though their sources and devices are many. (751)

A few lines later we are "near the solemn river, stealing away by night, as all things steal away, by night and by day, so quietly yielding to the attraction of the loadstone rock of Eternity . . ." (751). This reference too suggests the imminent death of Wrayburn and is overtly so connected by the narrative, but the death to come is Headstone's instead. However, no matter how immediately applicable, these passages reveal the cosmic moral background against which Dickens plays out his water music.[14] These passages also constitute instructions for the proper deciphering of the redundant information concerning water, but also indicate that water references are interlocked with other images, themes, and narrative gestures.

If there is water, there is also dust. Dust is most obviously connected to the accumulation of wealth by unsavory means. But the dust mounds in the story also represent the past as either opportunity or burden for the living. The Boffins benefit from old Harmon's will and acquire the mounds along with the estate. John Harmon rejects the imposition of the past upon him and frees himself from its dusty entrapment.[15] But the mounds themselves and dust in general also suggest mystery, and occlusion. When Lightwood makes the off-hand remark to Boffin that "everything wears to rags," Boffin replies "there's some things that I never found among the dust" (91). Boffin is called the Golden Dustman because for him the dust has meant great wealth, but he can put it in perspective and has come to the Temple "as a spot where lawyer's dust is contracted for . . ." (91). What is not found in the dust is unselfishness and love.[16] And just as the motif of recovery is associated with water, that of unburying and recovering is also associated with the dust, most particularly in the plotting of Wegg and Venus. That the accumulation of dust signifies a pernicious activity becomes evident when the narrator uses metaphors to castigate the authorities who have made the poor laws what they are.

> My lords and gentlemen and honourable boards, when you in the course of your dust-shovelling and cinder-raking have piled up a mountain of preten-

tious failure, you must off with your honourable coats for the removal of it, and fall to the work with the power of all the queen's horses and all the queen's men, or it will come rushing down and bury us alive. (503)

Those concluding words cannot help but remind us, as does Lightwood's remark that everything wears to rags, of the most famous quotation about dust—"dust thou art." Lest we forget that dimension, the narrator occasionally reminds us of it; thus, near the beginning of chapter 15, we find a paragraph beginning: "A grey dusty withered evening in London city has not a hopeful aspect. The closed warehouses and offices have an air of death about them, and the national dread of colour has an air of mourning" (393). The removal of the dust mounds, from this perspective, is a removal of all that is allied with the unattractiveness of death and the influence of the dead upon the living, including the will of a dead parent, but also of social conventions upon individuals.

The ooze, scum, mud, and slime associated with the corpses in the Thames, but also with Gaffer's own death and those of Headstone and Riderhood, call attention to the serious theme of mixing water and dust, or hidden forces and the unsavory accumulation of "wealth." Gaffer is driven by greed in his marginally legal trade; John Harmon Sr. is miserly in his assembling of the mounds. When these two metaphorical patterns come together, they suggest the ancient slime in which the predatory alligators and birds of prey live. But there is a lighter side to this pattern as well. It takes its climactic form with Silas Wegg, who has sought to acquire wealth through blackmailing Boffin about ownership of the dust mounds. John Harmon denounces Wegg as a "mudworm" at the moment of his unmasking (788). Like the other predators, this one too has failed. His fate is not as dramatic as Gaffer's, Headstone's, or Riderhood's, but it is related. Sloppy picks Wegg up and carries him into the street where he pitches him into a "scavenger's cart" where he makes "a prodigious splash" (790). It might not be the pit of a lock on the Thames, but it is ooze of a very disagreeable nature. Scavengers in the streets carried on a more reputable trade related to Gaffer's occupation. What were called dust carts collected animal and sometimes human waste as well. Wegg's removal from the narrative is prepared for long before when Jenny Wren tells her prodigal father, "'I'd give the dustman five shillings to carry you off in the dust cart'" (532), and in the foreign gentleman's misunderstanding about the "signs" on the London streets. The resolution to the problem of mud is hinted at in the scene of John and Bella's wedding, which takes place at Greenwich Church. Their air of happiness as they move off to the ceremony "wafted up from the earth and drew up after them a gruff and glum old pensioner" with two wooden legs and no object in life but tobacco.

"Stranded was Gruff and Glum in a harbour of everlasting mud, when all in an instant Bella floated him, and away he went" (664).[17] It is love and the prospect of domestic contentment that frees us from the selfishness and hopelessness of mud and slime.

I have argued thus far that Dickens has his narrator provide us with an excess of information about water in particular but also dust and mud to convey the central meaning of his complex narrative. I want now to argue that he employs this redundancy in order to maintain his own control of the narrative and to make as certain as possible that his text will not be mis-read.[18] We have already seen how Lightwood becomes a self-conscious narrator in the second chapter of the novel when he tells the story of the man from Somewhere. In chapter 16 of Book Two Lady Tippins recalls that it was during a dinner at the Veneerings that Lightwood first told the story of the man from Somewhere. Mortimer, again calling attention to the artificiality of narration, responds: "'Yes, Lady Tippins. . . . as they say on the stage, Even so!'" (411). We now learn that there is a sequel to that story, though Lightwood is reluctant to tell it until Wrayburn impatiently urges him to do so, declaring it insignificant and quoting a children's "narrative" to illustrate his point.

"I'll tell you a story
Of Jack a Manory,
And now my story's begun;
I'll tell you another
Of Jack and his brother,
And now my story is done." (412)

Wrayburn's poem suggests the inconsequentiality and lack of serious content in narratives, but Dickens's purpose here as elsewhere is to refute that claim. In fact, the sequel Lightwood has to tell is monumentally important to the narrative of *Our Mutual Friend,* for it involves an account of Riderhood's charges against Gaffer and his subsequent retraction of them, and climaxes with the information that Lizzie has vanished.

Lightwood can successfully minimize the importance of narrative in his first appearance as narrator; it is less easy to do so when his narrative involves his close friend Wrayburn, who is deeply concerned about Lizzie's disappearance, which sets him into action with very serious consequences. Lightwood's progress as a narrator suggests that any story might be far more important than we suppose. Who, as the party at the Veneerings entertained themselves with the story of a stranger, knew how intimately that story would intertwine with their own? But if the stories of strangers may prove surprisingly significant, false stories can be equally powerful. Riderhood's lying narrative about Gaffer must be expunged. The very subject of reading and interpretation must be examined. It can be elementary. Betty Higden explains that "'Sloppy is a beautiful reader of a newspaper. He do the Police in different voices'" (198). Reading, if it is only the conveying of information from the newspaper, requires some degree of interpretation. It is still the reception and translation of signs.

Of course, the central figures, when it comes to the theme of reading in this novel are Boffin and Wegg, the latter, as we have seen, concentrating almost parodically several of the serious themes of the novel. Boffin declares to Rokesmith, "I ain't a scholar in much, Rokesmith, but I'm a pretty fair scholar in dust," echoing Gaffer's boast that he is scholar enough to "read" the posters on his wall (185). In short, both men can "read" the signs of their trades. But Boffin is something more. Like Charley Hexam, he seeks to acquire the information stored in books and hires Wegg to assist him in this venture; Wegg himself, though literate, is not the scholar he pretends to be. Boffin wants to enjoy the fruits of literature, but soon finds himself in "severe literary difficulties" (178). The first mention of his "literary" difficulties actually pertains to his inability to keep his records straight. It is for this that he hires Rokesmith as secretary, though he realizes that employing Rokesmith will evoke jealousy in "'a literary man—with a wooden leg . . .'" (182). But there is another sense in which Boffin has literary difficulties. "What to believe, in the course of his reading, was Mr. Boffin's chief literary difficulty indeed . . ." (176). The written records he has listened to may provide historical truth, or simply be made-up tales. Without sufficient verification from many sources—another kind of redundancy—it is impossible to tell if a historical narrative is "true." But Boffin soon manifests yet another connection with literature. He shifts his reading from history to biography, and specifically the biographies of misers.[19] Seeming to accept these narratives as true accounts, he seeks out as many as he can in an attempt to validate the lifestyles of these men through a superfluous collection of information. We later learn that this is simply a ruse, but the ruse involves the transmitting of false signs for Wegg and Venus (and also Bella) to read—a kind of negative redundancy embedded in the larger narrative as a whole. Meanwhile, as he is sending these false signals, a "kind of illegibility" masks his own face (472). The once transparently readable Boffin has become a problem of interpretation. He is, in fact, creating a false narrative as potent as Riderhood's, though ultimately with a benign motive. For all that, it is still a lie. When is a lying narrative justified? When it leads to a happy ending? All fiction is, by definition, lying narrative, and Dickens made his living by it, so he had every reason to defend his own practice.

Boffin is not the only individual who is a text. In his passionate scene of declaration to and refusal by Lizzie, Headstone identifies "the text" that most deeply concerns him as "Mr. Eugene Wrayburn" (399). It is Wrayburn himself who delivers the riff on reading, by which the narrator makes this significant theme directly apparent. Wrayburn has just commented on Lightwood's "reading" of his weak character.

> (Bye-the-bye, that very word, Reading, in its critical use, always charms me. An actress's Reading of a chambermaid, a dancer's Reading of a hornpipe, a singer's Reading of a song, a marine painter's Reading of the sea, the kettle-drum's Reading of an instrumental passage, are phrases ever youthful and delightful.) (542)

If we hadn't figured it out before, this passage should help us to realize that reading is interpretation—the conversion of signs into expression, or the conversion of one set of signs into another, to be read in their turn by an audience of one sort or another. But what constitutes the appropriate material for an appropriate audience is often in doubt. In chapter 1 of Book Two entitled "Of an Educational Character," the narrator deplores the inappropriate narratives used in the first school Charley Hexam attends. Young women old in vices read the highly moralistic Adventures of Little Margery, and young dredgers and hulking mudlarks read the experiences of Thomas Twopence. The members of this audience require far other texts than these. The narrator opens the chapter with a significant statement about what constitutes education.

> The school at which young Charley Hexam had first learned from a book— the streets being, for pupils of his degree, the great preparatory Establish-ment in which very much that is never unlearned is learned without and before book—was a miserable loft in an unsavoury yard. (214)

You don't have to go to school to become a scholar of death posters or of dust. But you do have to "read" the signs around you and decode them accurately if you intend to survive.[20] This, of course, is the message of the novel's opening chapter.

Sometimes, however, it is necessary to read our own story before we try to interpret those of others. Hence, central to the narrative as a whole is a scene often regarded as clumsy by critics of this novel, in which John Harmon must tell himself his own story. Having left Pleasant Riderhood's shop, Harmon finds himself walking in circles in the unfamiliar neighbor-hood and complains to himself: "'This is like what I have read in narratives of escape from prison,' he said, 'where the little track of the fugitives in the night always seems to take the shape of the great round world on which they wander; as if it were a secret law'" (364). Soon, however, Harmon sets about his own narration, which is about an escape not from prison but from death by drowning. This act of narrating to himself, might seem redundant, since one would suppose no one knows more about oneself than oneself. But such an assumption can be mistaken, as Bella's case demonstrates. Harmon must reexamine his experience and read the signs anew from a changed perspective, something the narrator is constantly urging upon his readers. Thus Harmon's narration is a model within the larger narrative of how to process data so that it becomes information containing meaning upon which to act.[21] And act he does. At the end of this chapter Harmon declares his devotion for Bella and she rejects it, determining him to keep John Harmon down and let him remain dead. But, though readers are not privy to the fact, Harmon/Rokesmith has set a "secret law" in motion which will change the story of Bella's life. She has disliked being written into a role through the will of old John Harmon, but has focused on marriage for wealth as the object of her existence. Her fantasies about ships bringing in a rich husband and carrying out Bella married to one are her projection of her life story. But these projections are wrong and she marries the "poor" Rokesmith instead. After the revelation of Rokesmith's true identity, Mrs. Boffin concludes: "'and here you are, and the horses is in, and the story is done, and God bless you, my beauty, and God bless us all'" (774). But Bella is not content with this narrative and asks, "'But is the story done?'" and goes on to declare that she does not believe in Boffin's miserliness, but that he took on such a role to force her into recognizing her better self, an account closer to the truth (774).

Harmon has told himself his life story and thereby empowered himself to rewrite Bella's so that they both conclude with a happy ending. Boffin's role playing was intended to misinform Wegg and thereby lead him to overreach himself, but it has had the additional benefit of teaching Bella her true self. She has been rescued by Harmon in a far subtler way than Lizzie rescues Wrayburn, but there is an interesting connection between the two cases. At one point Jenny interrogates Lizzie about her feelings for Wrayburn, and, in her familiar manner, she finds her own love story in "the hollow down by the flare" in the fireplace (348). Like Harmon, she tells herself her own story, but as she tells it, it is a hopeless projection into the future, for this love story involves a lady not a waterman's daughter as the devoted companion to Wrayburn. Still, Lizzie, unknown to herself, has read the signs aright. She will end not only as Mrs. Wrayburn, but as Twemlow asserts, a lady as well.[22]

To a great extent *Our Mutual Friend* is about being able to tell ourselves our own life stories by correctly interpreting the signs. The novel is filled with characters who tell false tales for selfish ends—Wegg is a notable example, but the Lammles and Fledgeby are instances as well. Lightwood, Wrayburn, and Twemlow see no life stories for themselves, each being dominated, as John Harmon refuses to be, by a patriarchal directive. A realistic novel would be content to produce its narrative and perhaps allow the mirroring and contrasting of character types—a mode of redundancy too. But Dickens has embedded his redundancy not only in characterization and plotting, but in his very style, so that literal descriptions and figurative passages blend to convey an ever-increasing stream of data building to an inescapable message, though that message can only be read when all the signs the narrator has sent have been received. It seems to me that Dickens, though he could not use the language of information theory, intuitively understood the nature of his endeavor and how it differed from what was coming to be defined as realism. Part of his reason for resisting the conventions of realism, was his desire to retain control of his own narrative. As George Levine and others have suggested, to be true to itself realism had to have the appearance of not being tightly structured, since real life itself was perceived, in the realist worldview, not to be so structured (11). But Dickens, while he embraced the detailed recording of the material world in the manner of the realists, was not comfortable with the mode of realism. He wanted a world more intense than real life and yet potentially more under control, hence his famous remark to Wilkie Collins that a novelist resembles providence.[23] Dickens's late fiction can be likened to the late operas of Richard Wagner. Other musicians had used musical motifs to reinforce a "meaning" in their music, but Wagner so developed the concept of the musical motif that it became a language in its own right, and his operas were correctly "readable" only by those who had mastered the recurrent, varying, and interlocking motifs into a highly overdetermined design. Wagner's operas benefit from the concept of redundancy in music as *Our Mutual Friend* does, I believe, in fiction.

That Dickens knew full well how his use of redundancy with its proliferation of signs worked, his Postscript to the novel indicates. Some readers and commentators, he says, suppose that he was trying to conceal the fact that Rokesmith was Harmon, whereas that is what he was encouraging his readers to discover; it is, he writes, "in the interests of art, to hint to an audience that an artist (of whatever denomination) may perhaps be trusted to know what he is about in his vocation, if they will concede him a little patience. . . . To keep for a long time unsuspected, yet always working itself out, another purpose originating in that leading incident, and turning it to a pleasant and useful account at last, was the most interesting and the most difficult part of my design" (821). This difficulty is increased because one cannot expect that serial readers "will, until they have it before them complete, perceive the relations of its finer threads to the whole pattern which is always before the eyes of the story-weaver at his loom" (821). What I have tried to do in this chapter is to look at Dickens's often-examined narrative from a somewhat novel perspective in order that those finer threads might be more clearly discerned.

CONCLUSION

s Darío Villanueva has pointed out, realism can be
viewed in many ways. It may be a worldview, an object
of theoretical reflection, or a kind of art. At least since
Plato, art forms have been seen as attempts at mimesis,
the representation of actual existence. The trouble is that first we have
to decide what reality is and then attempt to represent it. For Plato, the
real was not necessarily the visible. The same was true for most medieval
Europeans, where the spiritual was real and physical phenomena were
transient. In Browning's "Fra Lippo Lippi," the painter has mastered
what we would call realism; he has held the mirror up to nature. But his
superiors in the church disapprove, suggesting that a focus on physical
details distracts one from the real purpose of art, which is to evoke the
spiritual. Giotto is recommended to him as a model. So determining
what is real is not as easy as it may seem.

Also, there is a difference between representing what is real and
what is true. Again, for many people in many places and times physical
appearances are an illusion and only the ideal is true. So, even in nineteenth-century England an author might feel she was writing the truth,
though not depicting the world around her in realistic terms. We must
also distinguish sincere writing from realistic writing. Any writer might
be sincere, true, and realistic at the same time, but these various qualities
may occur separately and be rendered by different manners.

The realism I refer to in this study is limited to the literary and artistic
approach that emerged in the West in the latter half of the nineteenth

century. Villanueva makes the distinction between genetic realism, which assumes an external reality that can be objectively captured, and formal realism, which is more concerned with the relationship of the author and his text. For literary critics and creative writers today, both forms of realism involve creating the illusion of reality. But with nineteenth-century realism, writers and artists sought to pass that illusion off as a correct reflection of the way things are. My argument here is that Dickens did not accept that program. If one likes, one could say that he preferred the true to the real. He wanted to emphasize the human capacity to imagine. He wanted to heighten human experience through fancy.

In this short study I have tried to show that Dickens behaved like a maestro. He was the one in control; he directed the way his readers' imaginations should go. He wanted his art to show ultimately, if not immediately. In his early writing he was willing to expose his tricks directly, but he became more and more crafty in both senses of the word as he matured, until in his late works he purposely masked clues to a correct reading of his narratives. What I have done is to offer some evidence for his consciousness of this program by exploring his use of such nonrealist devices as personification, first-person narration, and typical or symbolic naming, but also by studying the way he uses realist techniques such as description, metonymy, and redundancy in a way that subverts or directly opposes the realist use of these techniques. Dickens's descriptions, metonymies, and redundancies reinforce his command over the reader, whereas the realist seeks to give the reader a sense that she is controlling her reading. If Dickens could tell Wilkie Collins that the writer in some ways imitated providence, in his own writing he often sought to become that providential power that creates the design, makes his subjects follow it, and discloses its form when it has been fulfilled. What is interesting to me is the incredibly skillful methods he employed to do this, and I hope I have illuminated some of them here.

NOTES

Introduction

1. Not everyone saw Dickens as a realist in the years before the term became commonplace. In an 1851 review, David Masson put Thackeray in the real school and Dickens in the ideal (Hawes, 137).

2. Jane Millgate places Scott in the Romantic tradition, but in a way that aligns him with Dickens's outlook. She writes that "in the movement from verse romance to prose fiction as embodied in the completed *Waverley* of 1814, Scott shifts from an initial romanticism of a very eighteenth-century kind to that much more nineteenth-century variety which perceives the imagination not as the enemy of knowledge and wisdom but as their very source" (57).

3. Lukács connects Dickens to realism through his criticism of capitalism in *Dombey and Son* (212).

4. In the 70s, Maurice Larkin linked realism with a greater concern for material reality as shaper of man, with an emphasis on such concepts as determinism, heredity, and environment (2ff). Such an approach suggests a different notion of realism (it does set out to mirror nature) than Franklin's.

5. Barthes discusses these traits of writing in *S/Z* (4).

6. I am certainly not alone in seeing Gaskell and Dickens in opposition in the matter of literary realism. Here is a passage from Laurence Lerner's introduction to *Wives and Daughters*. "Like all realists, Elizabeth Gaskell believed that environment forms character. No novelist would meticulously create the social medium in which his characters move and have their being if he did not believe it mattered. The romantic is more likely to see personality as formed, mysteriously, from within; nothing makes it clearer that Dickens was not, at the deepest level, a realist, than the metaphysical exemption from social influence that he gives to his really good and his really evil characters" (26).

Chapter 1

1. I wish to thank James Phelan and Audrey Jaffe for their advice that helped me to clarify the argument of this essay and also audiences at Wayne State University and the University of Minnesota, Minneapolis, for their helpful questions and comments.

2. This quotation is taken from Dickens's preface to the Cheap Edition of *Oliver Twist* [1850], reprinted in the Clarendon Press edition 383.

3. He reasserted its existence in the preface to the Charles Dickens Edition of the novel in 1867.

4. But this dispute overlooks a more intriguing point that Umberto Eco explores in ".The Strange Case of the Rue Servandoni." This essay in *Six Walks in the Fictional Woods* asks, in Eco's own words: "What happens when in a fictional text the author posits, as an element of the actual world (which is the background of the fictional one) something that does not obtain in the actual world?" (100). More specifically, he is concerned with what happens when Alexander Dumas locates a clearly fictional place in a real historical setting—a certain street, for example, in seventeenth-century Paris. What difference does this make to the act of reading on the one hand, and what difference to the "real world" on the other? Though Eco touches briefly on the latter point, his real concern is with "the format of the model reader's Encyclopedia," his or her body of information available for interpreting *The Three Musketeers* (109).

5. Childers may be undervaluing the political project of deconstruction and over-simplifying the dismissal of written texts out of the realm of direct influence on the social realm, but he is not alone in his reaction. In a related approach, Gerald Dawson argues in *Soldier Heroes* that identity itself follows a similar pattern of agency. "As imagined forms, masculinities are at once 'made up' by creative cultural activity and yet materialize in the social world as structured forms with real effects upon both men and women" (22). Many commentators on deconstruction and postmodernism emphasize the movement away from the "real" toward the claustrophobia of the text. Christopher Norris offers this description of the trajectory from Foucault to Lyotard, Baudrillard, and the "apostles of postmodernity."

> As reality dissolved into the structures of discursive or textual representa-
> tion, so the subject (after Lacan: the "subject-presumed-to-know") became
> just a locus of multiple shifting and transient subject-positions, or a spec-
> ular reflex of the epistemic will-to-truth whose ubiquitous workings Fou-
> cault set out to expose. And from here it was no great distance to that stance
> of out-and-out cognitive scepticism—joined to an ultra-relativist position
> on issues of ethico-political judgment—which forms such a prominent
> (and depressing) feature of the current postmodernist cultural scene. (30)

Some time ago Terry Eagleton described the shift from structuralism to post-structuralism as "a shift from seeing the poem or novel as a closed entity, equipped with definite meanings which it is the critic's task to decipher, to seeing it as irreducibly plural, an endless play of signifiers which can never be finally nailed down to a single centre, essence or meaning" (138). Jonathan Culler's description of this same shift has a slightly different emphasis, but still stresses the increasing movement away from an acceptance of the text as referent to a "real" world and toward an emphasis upon the action of the text in and upon itself.

In simplest terms, structuralists take linguistics as a model and attempt to develop "grammars"—systematic inventories of elements and their possibilities of combination—that would account for the form and meaning of literary works; post-structuralists investigate the way in which this project is subverted by the workings of the texts themselves. Structuralists are convinced that systematic knowledge is possible; post-structuralists claim to know only the impossibility of this knowledge. (22)

6. Whether we see Dickens in the realist tradition or in some intermediary mode between romance and realism, it is pretty clear that he shared certain aims with novelists of his time. As Michael Irwin writes in his study of description in nineteenth-century fiction, "[t]he typical Victorian novel requires you to look for significance in terms of a slowly emerging pattern of relationships between an immense variety of elements, some important, some trivial, some the product of the intellect, some of imaginative instinct. It says more because it contains more. The author may fall short of his conscious purpose, but he may also exceed it. In showing how he looks at the world about him he is likely to betray limitations and prejudices—who would not? But he also projects a view of life" (157). In projecting that view of life, most Victorian writers sought to affect the views of their readers as well.

7. F. S. Schwarzbach writes of the detailed journey made by Oliver and the Artful Dodger into London.

The details of their route are scrupulously accurate—every street and turning is carefully and exactly named. And yet the effect is not, as one might expect, an enhanced sense of realism. The seeming precision is only on the surface: by naming the streets, and giving us no other detail about or description of them, the passage shatters their particularity and renders them virtually interchangeable. Reading the paragraph is like entering a maze, which is precisely what Oliver has done. This is the labyrinth of London. (46)

8. I would like to endorse Ruth Ronen's purpose of correcting the almost canonical theoretical perception of description as non-narrative. Along the way, she notes that description may serve many different narrative purposes. She describes description as "the territory of maximal reference and minimal significance" and notes that "the referentiality of descriptions, which is in itself a discursive convention, makes them generally devoid of meaning unless organized on a higher level" (282). With Dickens that organization took place consciously at the ideological level.

9. Carole Fabricant's *Swift's Landscapes* examines in detail Swift's idiosyncratic representation of real places, but does not pursue to any degree the philosophical or linguistic implications of his approach.

10. Richard Maxwell quotes a description of Jacob's Island from the *South London Chronicle* of 1 April 1890, indicating that the location's reputation persisted. Maxwell himself comments: "The willful mixing of rumor and fact is typical of Jacob's Island, a freak socially marginal to the great city yet strongly insistent, pulling the wanderer toward it" (90). In a footnote, Maxwell points out that Jacob's Island became identified with Dickens over the years. A celebration of the repeal of the Corn Laws was held in 1846 "on that highly interesting Spot, described by Charles Dickens." A newspaper

clipping of 1920 remarks that "the only visitors [Jacob's Island] receives from the outer world are the Dickensians. . . ." And a 1934 *Daily Mirror* article announced the demolition of Bill Sikes's house on Jacob's Island (Maxwell 341). Writing in the nineteen-forties, E. Beresford Chancellor was confident about Sikes's house: "The actual house visited by Sikes has been identified as being at the back of 18 Eckell Street in Metcalf Yard, now used as stables" (123). He offers no evidence for the identification. Not only is Jacob's Island identified with Dickens, but the expression "Dickensian," when applied to descriptions of certain kinds of poverty, tends to render them picturesque.

11. Wells's directions place Moreau's island in the region of the Galapagos Islands. Since Wells's novel deals with the attempt to speed up Darwinian speciation by surgical means, his directions for the island's location might have a sly, ironic point to make, something quite characteristic of the early Wells.

12. Lopes's *Foregrounded Description in Prose Fiction* makes a case for description's potential for major narrative functions, instead of consigning it to an inevitable background or subordinate role, as rhetorical tradition generally has done.

13. I can appreciate the pleasure derived from constructing a spatial design of the locations contained in a novel or in viewing such a design, but this is surely a pleasure separate from that of reading the text itself.

14. Another variation on the *Old Curiosity Shop* syndrome occurred when the *Bookman* ran a special number on Mrs. Humphry Ward and included photographs of real homes that presumably were the originals for the estates described in Ward's novels. This attempt to "authenticate" Ward's fictions offers little that is helpful in the way of appreciating her achievement as a novelist, though it may reveal a great deal about how readers conflate authors and their texts, often with less interest in the text than in the author's relationship to a presumed reality. The information about Ward and the *Bookman* I have derived from a paper by Beth Sutton Ramspeck entitled "A Photo's Worth a Dozen Novels? Mary Ward in Turn-of-the-Century Gaze" at the Midwest Victorian Studies Association conference at Indiana University, April 27, 1996.

15. In *Intentionality: An Essay in the Philosophy of Mind,* Searle explores in detail the underlying assumptions that support his view of intentionality.

Chapter 2

1. This chapter originated as a short essay by Susan Beckwith. I became a co-author and made extensive contributions to the original essay. Subsequently, I revised a good deal for inclusion in this book.

2. Lorna Martens's *The Diary Novel* examines this use of present-tense narration. The present tense was also often used clumsily to increase dramatic effect. In John Henry Newman's *Callista*, for example, there are many awkward shifts in tense where Newman seems merely to be attempting to heighten dramatic effect. Chapter 35 opens with the sentence: "We have already had occasion to mention that there were many secret well-wishers, or at least protectors of Christians, as in the world at large, so also in Sicca" (343). The next paragraph begins: "The burning sun of Africa is at the height of its power" (344). But the next is back to standard past-tense narration: "She too thought it was the unwelcome philosopher come again . . ." (344).

3. Janice Carlisle similarly notes that unconventional present-tense narration became commonplace in the late Victorian period especially among second-rate or

inexperienced writers (84).

4. Janice Carlisle and Randolph Quirk are two Dickens scholars who have noted Dickens's use of present tense. Carlisle sees its use in *Dombey and Son* as a means of achieving immediacy by drawing the reader more forcefully into the narrative (77, 85).

5. Early studies that concentrate on the relationships between providence and narrative include Leopold Damrosch Jr.'s *God's Plots and Man's Stories,* Thomas Vargish's *The Providential Aesthetic in Victorian Fiction,* and John R. Reed's *Victorian Will.* These scholars examine how writers of the eighteenth and nineteenth centuries in Great Britain and elsewhere could assume on their readers' part a belief in a covert and sometimes apparent teleology in human affairs under the superintendence of a benign or baleful God. In many instances, novelists likened their own plots to the implicit tendency of Providence.

6. Sue Lonoff notes this peculiar reader response in *Wilkie Collins and His Victorian Readers* (144).

7. This technique may serve two purposes: Rosemary Jann writes that "although authors using third-person narrators can accomplish this by limiting their omniscience, there is always a certain amount of conscious concealment of important information on the author's part that may try the reader's patience" (23), and Tzvetan Todorov points out, with respect to his formulation of point of view, that "the tenor of each piece of information is determined by the person who transmits it, no observation exists without an observer" (46). Thus Collins's use of several first-person narrators also serves to disguise any objective truth that an omniscient narrator would have to provide; the eyewitnesses who speak for themselves may distort a clue that is the key to the mystery. However, should this happen within Collins's structure of the narrative, neither the "editor" nor the author would be held to blame for this misinterpretation.

8. Martens deals with this particular point in her excellent examination of diary writing (5), but, oddly enough, though she mentions Miss Clack's diary in *The Moonstone,* she entirely overlooks the more dramatic instance of Marian Halcombe's in *The Woman in White.*

9. It is also possible for the diarist to record recollections and memories of more distant pasts. And, as an aside, I should also note that diarists record not only their own stories, but the lives (past and present) of those around them.

10. But what does it mean to end well? Where is the end that is well? Frank Kermode emphasizes in *The Genesis of Secrecy* that human life is played out with a sense that we are in the middle of events. He addresses this issue on the cosmic level, but it applies as well to individual lives. The person who writes an autobiography at the age of thirty comes to the end of things in her narrative and might even conclude that the story of her life has ended well. But the next few years might change that story considerably.

11. Although it is only tangential to my interests here, it is a note of some importance that Marian never speaks for herself outside of the medium of the diary. Hereafter, anything which she contributes is filtered through Hartright's narrative.

12. Dickens used present-tense narration elsewhere—in *Dombey and Son* and *David Copperfield,* for example—but his use of present tense in the three novels discussed here is systematic and extensive.

13. Carlyle made frequent use of present tense narration in *The French Revolution,* thereby creating greater drama and what he himself regarded as a novelistic effect. Of course, Dickens claimed to have read *The French Revolution* many times and declared it a source for his own *A Tale of Two Cities.*

14. An extreme example of this penetration in cinema is *Last Year at Marienbad,* written by Alain Robbe-Grillet and directed by Alain Resnais.

15. What I am describing here using Benveniste's terms, Suzanne Fleishman explores in narratological terms, explaining that present-tense narrations are unstable because they erase the distinction between the two temporal planes of the past tense of narrated events and the time of narration.

16. Shlomith Rimmon-Kenan accepts the idea of external and internal focalization (74ff).

17. See Genette's response to Bal in *Narrative Discourse Revisited,* chapter 12. Seymour Chatman offers different terms to clarify the process others lump together as focalization. "I propose slant to name the narrator's attitudes and other mental nuances appropriate to the report function of discourse, and filter to name the much wider range of mental activity experienced by characters in the story world—perceptions, cognitions, attitudes, emotions, memories, fantasies, and the like" (143). Manfred Jahn offers a means to adjust this difference within the concept of focalization by employing the concept of field of vision and presenting the idea of narrators at the windows of James's House of Fiction.

18. Another notorious instance is in chapter 32, when the narrator associates Krook's spontaneous combustion with the injustice of the British courts.

19. Of the 23 chapters, those already mentioned as well as those numbered 9, 10, 11, 13, 15, 16, 17, 18, 20, 21, and 22 are in the past tense. The novel opens and closes (though we can never know if the later action would have been Dickens's intent) with a present-tense narration.

20. It would be interesting to consider the situation of the "implied" audience. This chapter deals only with the fact that Dickens has set up a narrative that is being told in the present tense by an unknown narrator. But to whom is this narrator speaking, for this is speech and not written text? Does not the present-tense narrator imply an immediate present-tense auditor? The device that this most immediately resembles is the aside spoken by a living actor to a living audience in the theater, and there is no question but that Dickens's use of present-tense narration in *Drood* heightens the drama. Several authors have dealt with problems of audience reception of present-tense narration from Genette on, but one of the most compelling is James Phelan's study of J. M. Coetzee's *Waiting for the Barbarians,* where the instability created by simultaneous narration acts as a means of involving the reader in a double sense of complicity, first in the events of the story and then in the way that we are obliged to process them.

21. Robin W. Winks makes a similar comparison in *Modus Operandi,* when he states that "In football . . . the variables at any given moment are enormous. To the spectator, suspense arises as much from not knowing what must happen next . . .—the huddle allows one's doubts, like private detectives, to search out weaknesses in the game plan . . . the beauty in sport . . . arises from the persistence of doubt, and its mounting repetitious nature . . . living with ambiguity is not easy. Most people like their History [*sic*] clear and plain" (8). In the Victorian era the variables themselves were not even fully known and history was being eroded by a new revolution—one which questioned not just the structures, but the very foundations upon which people laid their lives.

22. Morson unwittingly supports this picture of the serial reader when he says, "spectators have to be *simultaneous* with the events they watch" (176). *The Mystery of Edwin Drood* dramatically confirms the open-endedness of serial publication because Dickens's death before the narrative was completed has turned the novel into a continuing memorial of such open-endedness.

Chapter 3

1. S. D. Powell calls attention to the well-established tradition of interest in Dickens's naming of characters in a long footnote, listing Elizabeth Hope Gordon as among the first to attempt to categorize those names (63).

2. Miller observes that this allusion to Halevy's aria compounds a pattern of other references to Jewishness, anti-Semitism, and so forth pervasive in Proust's narrative.

3. Harry Stone examines the intricacies of Dickens's practice of naming and calls it a "carefully calculated and artfully articulated system that gives up its secrets only to the initiate" ("What's in a Name?" 193). It is possible that naming had greater resonance in the nineteenth century than it does today, since naming was recognized as part of formal church practice. Michael Cotsell remarks in reference to a passage in *Our Mutual Friend* that the second question in the Catechism of the Church of England is "Who gave you this Name?", for which the answer is: "My Godfathers and Godmothers in my Baptism; wherein I was made a member of Christ, the child of God, and an inheritor of the kingdom of heaven" (173). The narrator makes direct reference to this situation in chapter 40 of *Bleak House,* when he notes that on the occasion of Woolwich's last birthday, "Mr. Bagnet certainly did, after observing on his growth and general advancement, proceed, in a moment of profound reflection on the changes wrought by time, to examine him in the catechism; accomplishing with extreme accuracy the questions number one and two, What is your name? And Who gave you that name? But there failing in the exact precision of his memory, and substituting for number three, the question And how do you like that name?" (666).

4. Harry Stone examines the significance of Headstone's name in some detail ("What's in a Name" 198ff). Joel Brattin offers a close look at Headstone's name and more by way of a reading of Dickens's manuscript (147ff).

5. Viewing naming as an assertion of power is my suggestion, not Stewart's.

6. Michael Cotsell reminds us that Jenny Wren is a character out of nursery lore, notably as the partner of Robin Redbreast or Cock Robin. He reproduces a poem in which Jenny Wren falls sick and gets well, but is hostile to Robin Redbreast (140).

7. *David Copperfield* has attracted the most attention about naming among Dickens's novels. I refer here to two recent articles, one by S. D. Powell and one by Richard Lettis, both of which appeared together in *Dickens Studies Annual.*

8. Richard Lettis says that Brooks is a conventional British alias (75).

9. S. D. Powell has this to say about Dora's nickname for David:

> His willing acceptance of this name, however, and the narrator's refusal to criticize himself for it, should be an immediate tip-off that his attraction to Dora is wrongheaded, that the narrator recognizes as we do that "Doady" represents a step back from the mature freedom of "Trotwood" and the family that bestowed that name. (56–57)

10. Richard Lettis comments that nobody knows Littimer's Christian name (71).

11. Harry Stone shows how Dickens fits Murdstone into a similar larger pattern.

> "The notes, therefore, not only show Dickens carefully fashioning the name 'Murdstone,' but shaping the name and controlling the attendant imagery (and the motifs that the name and the imagery embody) so that each

enriches and illuminates the other." ("What's in a Name?" 196)

12. I find J. Hillis Miller's reading of *Bleak House* compatible with my argument about Dickens's mode of incorporating his names into a larger network of imagery.

> *Bleak House* is properly allegorical, according to a definition of allegory as a temporal system of cross references among signs rather than as a spatial pattern of correspondence between signs and referents. Most people in the novel live without understanding their plight. The novel, on the other hand, gives the reader the information necessary to understand why the characters suffer, and at the same time the power to understand that the novel is fiction rather than mimesis. The novel calls attention to its own procedures and confesses to its own rhetoric, not only, for example, in the onomastic system of metaphorical names already discussed, but also in the insistent metaphors of the style throughout. (Introduction 29)

13. Juliet McMaster observes an interesting pattern of naming in *The Old Curiosity Shop*. Whereas there is detailed naming in Quilp's side of the narrative, the naming is intentionally vague and general in Nell's, in keeping, she suggests, with the interests of a "generalized allegorical fable" (114). She also comments on Quilp's fascination with naming as an "almost fiendish device" (115).

14. Tom Lloyd examines some of the consequences of names in regard to Pip and Magwitch (104ff).

15. Cotsell notes that Dickens was given to this kind of naming, especially for voting constituencies—the most memorable, perhaps, being the town of Eatanswill in *Pickwick Papers* (144).

16. McMaster, again, notes that place names are particular where associated with Quilp, but unspecific when associated with Nell (116). Dickens uses a far different approach in *Hard Times*, beginning with the appropriate Coketown for the name of its chief city.

17. Harry Stone does not highlight the difference between Dickens's aims in writing and those of the realists, but his description of those aims is highly compatible with my own.

> What then can we conclude from the process I have just been tracing? Simply this: that Dickens's names are quintessential embodiments of what one sees everywhere in his art, a fusion of the wild, the portentous, and the fantastic with the rational and the everyday. His names, like his whispering houses, terrifying streets, primordial storms, and spell-casting witches are at once wildly expressionistic and improbable and profoundly real and ordinary. Dickens conveys with the same stroke the surface of things and the hidden springs of meaning. His world is discrete, tangible, and familiar, but also interconnected, fantastic, and mysterious. ("What's in a Name" 203)

Chapter 4

1. Juliet McMasters mentions the leitmotif of handkerchiefs in the novel, including

Bill Sikes's handkerchief that foreshadows his accidental hanging (47ff). John O. Jordan indicates that Dickens is true to the facts of his time in his "sociological" treatment of handkerchiefs, but also suggests that Dickens goes beyond realism. "As they reappear and pass from one context to another, handkerchiefs take on increasing thematic and figural significance in the novel" (6). It is just this movement from the real to the figural that I am arguing Dickens became conscious of and used more and more purposefully through his career.

2. I offer a different approach to the description of Jacob's Island in chapter 1 of the present study.

3. Jakobson makes this distinction about literature, but his study of contiguous (metonymic) and similar (metaphoric) patterns of thinking and linguistic expression is based upon the clinical study of aphasia.

4. As mentioned in the text, J. Hillis Miller provides an excellent study of "Meditations in Monmouth Street" as a mode of metonymic description and then later indicates how this remarkable performance is based upon a convention. "The row of old clothes which Boz sees in Monmouth Street gives rise, however, to a wholly conventional narrative, the story of the idle apprentice" (*Sketches* 35).

5. Nancy Aycock Metz calls attention to the Analytical's relationship to the narrator.

6. Although I admire Kearns's arguments, I think that they are undermined to a large degree by the works that she chooses to treat as realist texts. Although she herself suggests that *Frankenstein, A Blithedale Romance, Wuthering Heights,* and much of Dickens do not really represent realism, she goes on to explore these works in detail. Moreover, she includes *Dracula* in the range of realism!

7. Miller contends against Jakobson's opposition of metonymy/prose vs metaphor/poetry, declaring there can be no such diagrammatic opposition (40). But Jakobson is not so hard and fast as Miller suggests, indicating that metonymy and metaphor are polarities on a continuum.

Chapter 5

1. Susan Horton captures this aspect of Dickens's writing:

> There comes to be in the reader of Dickens's novels, then, a powerful perception of meaning at the point at which the reader begins to see gestural, phrasal, behavioural predictability in Dickens's fictive world run directly up against Dickens's world in description, which turns out to be a world in flux, and always and ever in the process of transformation. (8)

2. J. Hillis Miller argues for a kind of utility for prosopopoeia, but as a speech act performed by an author/narrator, and an interpretation of that act by a reader, both of which result in making something happen. But I am speaking of the personifications within the diegesis—that is, the events and circumstances of the narrative.

3. Richard Lettis puts the tension in these terms.

> Faced with a choice between reality and imagination, Dickens usually chose the latter, but he distinguished between the imaginative and the ideal; obliged to choose between reality and unfounded ideality, he chose the real. (208)

4. Peter Brooks, like many other critics, is reluctant to classify Dickens as a realist, but finally includes *Hard Times* as a questionable example of the realist impulse, though he is disappointed in its lack of specific social detail. One of his observations about the novel fits in nicely with the passages I have cited from Horton and Kucich. He says that Dickens employs "the procedure of turning all issues, facts, conditions, into questions of style. *Hard Times* becomes, even more than Dickens's other novels, a drama of opposed styles, presided over by the quicksilver agility of the narrator's styles" (43–44). I would add to this that it is precisely through the mastery of style that Dickens retains control of his text in a way that realists cannot.

5. I discuss Dickens's nonrealist use of metonymy in chapter 4 of this study.

Chapter 6

1. Henry James, *The Art of Fiction and Other Essays* (New York: Oxford University Press, 1948), 49.

2. In "The Cup and the Lip and the Riddle of *Our Mutual Friend*," *ELH* 62:4 (1995), 955–77, Gregg A. Hecimovich discloses a particularly sophisticated riddling technique in the novel. My approach resembles his in calling attention to a need for interpreting clues, but my focus is far different, concentrating on the way in which Dickens swamps his reader with information initially seeming to be redundant in the colloquial sense, but ultimately helping to deliver the novel's meaning more clearly. Both Hecimovich and I agree on Dickens's purpose of wanting to reinforce the significance of his narrative.

3. George Levine in his seminal *The Realistic Imagination: English Fiction from* Frankenstein *to* Lady Chatterley (Chicago: University of Chicago Press, 1981) wrote that the realist effort was "the struggle to avoid the inevitable conventionality of language in pursuit of the unattainable unmediated reality. Realism, as a literary method, can in these terms be defined as a self-conscious effort, usually in the name of some moral enterprise of truth telling and extending the limits of human sympathy, to make literature appear to be describing directly not some other language but reality itself (whatever that may be taken to be): in this effort, the writer must self-contradictorily dismiss previous conventions of representation while, in effect, establishing new ones" (8). He also wrote that "the continuing literary problem that plagued realism from the start was the incompatibility of tight form with plausibility" (11). There is a long history in modern literary criticism of the interrogation of Victorian realism, beginning at least with Kenneth Graham's *English Criticism of the Novel 1865–1900*.

4. Information theory has found its way into so much of today's culture that an elaborate discussion of it here is unnecessary. It has even penetrated the natural sciences, affecting the discourse of such fields as genetics and microbiology, where there is much discussion about the transmission of "information" by chromosomal action. Friedrich Kittler demonstrates, in his essay "The World of the Symbolic," Jacque Lacan's use of information theory for psychoanalytic theory, and Umberto Eco, in *The Open Work*, applies what he prefers to call communication theory to music, making use of Leonard B. Meyer's "Meaning in Music and Information Theory." My understanding of information theory is derived largely from Jeremy Campbell's *Grammatical Man: Information, Entropy, Language, and Life*. Subsequent references appear in the text. Campbell gives an account of information theory based primarily upon the work of Claude

Shannon, but more recent theories provide some different perspectives on that work. Kittler quotes the following passage about what has been called "logical depth" at IBM.

> The value of a message . . . appears to reside not in its information (its absolutely unpredictable parts), nor in its obvious redundancy (verbatim repetitions, unequal digit frequencies), but rather in what may be called its buried redundancy—parts predictable only with difficulty, things the receiver could in principle have figured out without being told, but only at considerable cost in money, time, or computation. (152)

5. Charles Dickens, *Our Mutual Friend* (London: Oxford University Press, 1967), 1. Subsequent references appear in the text.

6. John Romano notes that Lightwood, in his first narration, is satirizing a specific kind of sentimental romance, but the story he tells nonetheless has real force (37). I can't agree with Romano's suggestion that Mortimer mirrors Dickens's own desire to discredit representational form, though I do agree that Dickens wishes to get beyond many conventions of the fiction of his day.

7. Redundancy is a notion familiar now in various areas of language and symbol study, such as linguistics and composition. A few examples include Jean-Claude Choul's "Redundancy as a Semiotic Principle," Alice Horning's "Readable Writing: The Role of Cohesion and Redundancy," and Susan Rubin Suleiman, "Redundancy and the 'Readable' Text."

8. This equation was invented by Ludwig Boltzmann; in it, S stands for entropy, k for a universal constant known as Boltzmann's constant, and W for the number of ways in which the system can be arranged (Campbell, 46).

9. Redundancy has been employed to examine literary techniques. Umberto Eco's *The Open Work* was an early example of its use in literary theory, and it shows up as well in Kittler's essays. However, the term, when applied to literary analysis, has varying meanings. James Phelan offers an illuminating approach, very different from my own, in his essay "Redundant Telling, Preserving the Mimetic, and the Functions of Character Narration," where he is concerned with the way in which an author must convey information to her readership which is redundant in her text. "Redundant telling occurs when a narrator gives an unmotivated report of information to a narratee that the narratee already possesses" (210). His examples are Browning's "My Last Duchess" and Sandra Cisneros's short story "Barbie-Q." Meir Sternberg uses the idea of redundancy as overwriting in *Expositional Modes and Temporal Order in Fiction* and *The Poetics of Biblical Narrative: Ideological Literature and the Drama of Reading*.

10. The conference involved scientists associated with MIT's new Neuroscience Research Project and featured Roman Jakobson, who suggested the similarity between linguistic and molecular codes.

11. Tom Lloyd writes of the handkerchief: "It is invested with different meanings, yet it means nothing in itself as it passes from person to person; thus, it is emblematic of the system of disengaged signs on which society rests in *Bleak House*. Esther's gift of the handkerchief is a selfless act; around it, the mother builds a shrine with its "little bunch of sweet herbs" (*BH* 162), but for Lady Dedlock it suggests the child she has "discovered yet buried" (10).

12. I have mentioned only a few examples of a pattern of redundancy that is quite complex. Just one additional example indicates how the death and burial theme reveals

through family history, violence, and supposed revenants, broad social and political implications. I refer to the whole assemblage of references to the Ghost's Walk at Chesney Wold.

13. If anyone should doubt that Dickens knew full well how he was tightly structuring his novel and keeping it under his own control, his notes for chapter 6 make his intentions clear. In *The Companion to* Our Mutual Friend, Michael Cotsell indicates that Dickens wrote: "Back to the opening chapter of the book. strongly," that last word underlined three times (255).

14. J. Hillis Miller sees the river as representing "material otherness" to human beings, to which the mysterious depth of the human spirit is analogous, in *Charles Dickens: The World of His Novels*, 318ff. He describes the river as a realm of death and transformation.

15. A complicated thematic pattern of captivity, imprisonment, and other forms of confinement winds its way through *Our Mutual Friend* to reinforce the same overall message stressed by those of water, dirt, and mud themes.

16. Michael Cotsell calls attention to a passage in the manuscript of *Friend* that is omitted in the proofs, which indicates that what is not found in the dust mounds is "what's good and true" (*Companion*, 75).

17. This scene interestingly brings together the water and earth motifs. Greenwich Hospital was the official retirement facility for invalids who had served in the Royal Navy. Gruff and Glum had obviously seen serious action, as his two wooden legs suggest, but he also hints at the mudworm Wegg with his one wooden leg. Unlike Wegg, the pensioner can be won over and raised up from the mud by the spectacle of love. Greenwich Hospital and the pensioner might have been in Dickens's mind because as he was completing *Our Mutual Friend,* an act of Parliament in 1865 allowed out-pensions to the pensioners, who would no longer be required to live on the grounds.

18. The concept of the death of the author, from Roland Barthes onward, along with the active fields of reader response and reception theory, among other critical approaches, necessarily plays down the masterfulness of the author. One imagines these theoretical approaches would have been anathema to a writer like Dickens, who exerted himself to retain as much control as he could over his texts, including his artist's illustrations for them.

19. Boffin's idealization of the lives of famous misers might be read as a playful inversion of Carlyle's assertion: "The history of the world is but the biography of great men."

20. Murray Baumgarten writes in "Fictions of the City," *The Cambridge Companion to Charles Dickens:* "Like the detectives of the London Metropolitan Police, founded in 1829, whom he admired and wrote about in *Household Words*, Dickens teaches us how to decode that city world and navigate through its darker streets. His fiction trains us in keen and swift observation, careful judgment, and thoughtful commitment" (117).

21. Eco reminds us that information theory was not designed for analyzing works of art, but his endeavor in *The Open Work* is to demonstrate that a work of art can be analyzed like any other form of communication and information theory can assist in that endeavor (68). Eco also states that the meaning of a message "is a function of the order, the conventions, and the redundancy of its structure. The more one respects the laws of probability (the preestablished principles that guide the organization of a message and are reiterated via the repetition of foreseeable elements), the clearer and less ambiguous its meaning will be" (93). My position in this chapter is that Dickens increases the likelihood of his message being conveyed by redundant thematic elements, even as he tests

some of the conventions of the novel form. Those who have seen *Our Mutual Friend* as a disordered baggy monster, have, in my view, missed the message.

22. The importance of underrating and of controlling narratives takes some odd little turns in the novel. For example, when Jenny's father discovers Lizzie's whereabouts, young Blight brings him to Wrayburn at the Veneerings'. He sends in a note to notify his master. This is an important turning point in the narrative, for Wrayburn will now pursue Lizzie and be pursued by Headstone. But there is a possibility that this line of action might be prevented and the narrator hints at it in a self-reflexive manner. "Then the Analytical, perusing a scrap of paper lying on the salver, with the air of a literary Censor, adjusts it, takes his time about going to the table with it, and presents it to Mr. Eugene Wrayburn" (627). Nancy Aycock Metz has suggested in "The Artistic Reclamation of Waste in *Our Mutual Friend*" that the Analytical Chemist mirrors the narrator in various ways. Here he could be considered as a force capable of redirecting the narrative by refusing to deliver the necessary data to generate Wrayburn's next actions. As elsewhere in the novel, he does not interfere with the tale.

23. Dickens wrote a now-famous letter to Wilkie Collins on 6 October 1859, in which he likened the novelist's role to that of providence. I am not arguing that Dickens had a simple perception of ordered existence. I believe he felt it necessary to fight for such an order. But this order had less to do with the conventions of realism than with the adventures of the imagination. John Romano puts the case rather well when he writes, "Dickens' own epistemology, if it may be called one, seems indeed to have been that reality is forever escaping our grasp, forever going deeper than, forever superseding and outdistancing, the forms provided by the chasing mind" (46–47).

BIBLIOGRAPHY

Ackerman, Jennifer. *Chance in the House of Fate: A Natural History of Heredity.* New York: Houghton Mifflin Co., 2001.

Alter, Robert. "Reading Style in Dickens." *Philosophy and Literature* 20, no. 1 (1996).

Bal, Mieke. *Narratology: Introduction to the Theory of Narrative,* translated by Christine van Boheemen. Toronto: University of Toronto Press, 1992.

Barthes, Roland. *S/Z,* translated by Richard Miller, Preface by Richard Howard. New York: Hill and Wang, 1974 [original publication in French, 1970].

Baumgarten, Murray. "Fictions of the City." *The Cambridge Companion to Charles Dickens,* edited John O. Jordan. Cambridge: Cambridge University Press, 2001. 106–19.

Benveniste, Emile. *Problems in General Linguistics,* translated by Mary Elizabeth Meek. Coral Gables, FL: University of Miami Press, 1971.

Brattin, "Dickens' Creation of Bradley Headstone." *Dickens Studies Annual: Essays on Victorian Fiction,* vol. 14, edited by Michael Timko, Fred Kaplan, and Edward Guiliano. New York: AMS Press, 1985. 147–65.

Brooks, Peter. *Realist Vision.* New Haven and London: Yale University Press, 2005.

Brooke-Rose, Christine, "Narrating without a Narrator." *Times Literary Supplement,* December 31, 1999: 1213.

Buck, Anne. *Victorian Costume and Costume Accessories,* rev. 2nd ed. Carlton, Bedford: Ruth Bean, 1984.

Campbell, Jeremy. *Grammatical Man: Information, Entropy, Language, and Life.* New York: Simon & Schuster, 1982.

Carlisle, Janice. *The Sense of an Audience: Dickens, Thackeray, and George Eliot at Mid-Century.* Athens: University of Georgia Press, 1981.

Casparis, Christian Paul. *Tense without Time: The Present Tense in Narration.* Bern: Francke Verlag, 1975.

Chancellor, E. Beresford. *The London of Charles Dickens.* New York: George H. Doran Co., n.d.

Chatman, Seymour. *Story and Discourse: Narrative Structure in Fiction and Film*. Ithaca: Cornell University Press, 1978.

Childers, Joseph W. *Novel Possibilities: Fiction and the Formation of Early Victorian Culture*. Philadelphia: University of Pennsylvania Press, 1995.

Choul, Jean-Claude. "Redundancy as a Semiotic Principle." *Semiotics 1984*, edited by John Deely. Lanham, MD: University Presses of America, 1985. 239–49.

Cohn, Dorrit. *The Distinction of Fiction*. Baltimore: Johns Hopkins University Press, 1999.

Collins, Wilkie. *The Woman in White*. Oxford: Oxford University Press, 1998.

Cotsell, Michael. *The Companion to* Our Mutual Friend. London: Allen & Unwin, 1986.

Culler, Jonathan. *On Deconstruction: Theory and Criticism after Structuralism*. Ithaca: Cornell University Press, 1982.

Cunnington, C. Willett, and Phillis Cunnington, illustrations by Phillis Cunnington, Cecil Everitt, and Catherine Lucas. *Handbook of English Costume in the Nineteenth Century*. London: Faber and Faber, 3rd ed., 1970 [Originally published 1959].

Damrosch, Leopold Jr. *God's Plots and Man's Stories: Studies in the Fictional Imagination from Milton to Fielding*. Chicago: University of Chicago Press, 1985.

Davis, Lennard J. *Resisting Novels: Ideology and Fiction*. New York: Methuen, 1987.

Dawson, Gerald. *Soldier Heroes: British Adventure, Empire and the Imagining of Masculinities*. London: Routledge, 1994.

Dickens, Charles. *Bleak House*. Oxford: Oxford University Press, 1966.

———. *Christmas Books*. New York: Oxford University Press, 1987.

———. *A Christmas Carol*, Christmas Books. Oxford: Oxford University Press, 1987.

———. *David Copperfield*. Oxford: Oxford University Press, 1960.

———. *Dombey and Son*. New York: Oxford University Press, 1960.

———. *Great Expectations*, edited by Angus Calder. Harmondsworth, England: Penguin Books, 1985.

———. *Hard Times*. Oxford: Oxford University Press, 1970.

———. *The Letters of Charles Dickens*, edited by Madeline House and Graham Storey. Oxford: The Clarendon Press, 1965.

———. *Little Dorrit*. New York: Oxford University Press, 1963.

———. *The Mystery of Edwin Drood*, edited by Margaret Cardwell. Oxford: The Clarendon Press, 1972.

———. *Oliver Twist*, edited by Kathleen Tillotson. Oxford: The Clarendon Press, 1966.

———. *Our Mutual Friend*. Oxford: Oxford University Press, 1967.

———. *The Pickwick Papers*. New York: Oxford University Press, 1967.

———. *Sketches by Boz*. London: Oxford University Press, 1963.

———. *The Speeches of Charles Dickens. A Complete Edition*, edited by K. J. Fielding. Atlantic Highlands, NJ: Harvester Wheatsheaf, 1988.

———. *The Uncommercial Traveler and Reprinted Pieces*. London: Oxford University Press, 1964.

Doyle, Sir Arthur Conan. *Memories and Adventures*. Boston: Little, Brown, 1924.

Eagleton, Terry. *Literary Theory: An Introduction*. Minneapolis: University of Minnesota Press, 1983.

Eco, Umberto. *The Open Work*, translated by Anna Cancogni. Cambridge: Harvard University Press, 1989.

———. *Six Walks in the Fictional Woods*. Cambridge: Harvard University Press, 1995.

———. *Travels in Hyperreality*, translated by William Weaver. New York: Harcourt

Brace & Co.; A Harvest Book, 1990.

Edgecomb, Rodney Stenning. "Personification in the Late Novels of Dickens." *Dickensian* 95, no. 3 (Winter 1999): 230–40.

Eigner, Edward M. *The Metaphysical Novel in England and America: Dickens, Bulwer, Hawthorne, and Melville*. Los Angeles: University of California Press, 1978.

Fabricant, Carole. *Swift's Landscapes*. South Bend: University of Notre Dame Press, 1992.

Fleischman, Suzanne. *Tense and Narrativity: From Medieval Performance to Modern Fiction*. Austin: University of Texas Press, 1990.

Ford, George H. *Dickens and His Readers: Aspects of Novel Criticism since 1836*. New York: W. W. Norton & Co., 1965.

Franklin, J. Jeffrey. *Serious Play: The Cultural Form of the Nineteenth-Century Realist Novel*. Philadelphia: University of Pennsylvania Press, 1999.

Furst, Lilian R. *All Is True: The Claims and Strategies of Realist Fiction*. Durham: Duke University Press, 1995.

Gallagher, Catherine. *Nobody's Story: The Vanishing Acts of Women Writers in the Marketplace, 1670–1820*. Berkeley: University of California Press, 1994.

Gaskell, Elizabeth. *Sylvia's Lovers,* edited by Andrew Sanders. New York: Oxford University Press, 1982.

———. *Wives and Daughters,* edited by Frank Glover Smith, Introduction by Laurence Lerner. Harmondsworth, Middlesex, England: Penguin Books Ltd., 1975 [Originally published 1864–66].

Genette, Gérard. *Fiction and Diction,* translated by Catherine Porter. Ithaca: Cornell University Press, 1993.

———. *Narrative Discourse Revisited,* translated by Jane E. Lewin. Ithaca: Cornell University Press, 1994.

Glavin, John. "Dickens and Theatre." *Cambridge Companion to Charles Dickens,* edited by John O. Jordan. Cambridge: Cambridge University Press, 2001.

Goodridge, J. Frank. "The Circumambient Universe," *Twentieth-Century Interpretations of* Wuthering Heights: *A Collection of Essays,* edited by Thomas A. Vogler. Englewood Cliffs, NJ: Prentice-Hall, 1968. 69–77.

Graham, Kenneth. *English Criticism of the Novel 1865–1900*. Oxford: The Clarendon Press, 1965.

Grillo, Virgil. *Charles Dickens' Sketches by Boz: End in the Beginning*. Boulder: The Colorado Associated University Press, 1974.

Hamon, Phillipe. "Rhetorical Status of the Descriptive." *Yale French Studies* 61 (1981): 1–26.

Hawes, Donald. *Charles Dickens*. London: Continuum, 2007.

Hecimovich, Gregg A. "The Cup and the Lip and the Riddle of *Our Mutual Friend*." *ELH* 62, no. 4 (1995).

Horning, Alice. "Readable Writing: The Role of Cohesion and Redundancy." *JAC: A Journal of Composition Theory* 11, no. 1 (Winter 1991): 135–45.

Horton, Susan. *The Reader in the Dickens World: Style and Response*. Pittsburgh: University of Pittsburgh Press, 1981.

Humphcrys, Anne. *Travels into the Poor Man's Country: The Work of Henry Mayhew*. Athens: University of Georgia Press, 1977.

Irwin, Michael. *Picturing: Description and Illusion in the Nineteenth-Century Novel*. London: George Allen & Unwin, 1979.

Iser, Wolfgang. *The Fictive and the Imaginary: Charting Literary Anthropology*. Baltimore: Johns Hopkins University Press, 1993.

Jahn, Manfred, "Windows of Focalization: Deconstructing and Reconstructing a Narratological Concept." *Style* 30, no. 2 (Summer 1996): 241–67.

Jakobson, Roman and Morris Halle. *Fundamentals of Language*. The Hague: Mouton, 1956.

James, Henry. *The Art of Fiction and Other Essays*. New York: Oxford University Press, 1948.

Jann, Rosemary. *The Adventures of Sherlock Holmes: Detecting Social Order*. New York: Twayne, 1995.

John, Juliet. *Dickens's Villains: Melodrama, Character, Popular Culture*. Oxford: Oxford University Press, 2001.

Jordan, John O. "'The Purloined Handkerchief.'" *Dickens Studies Annual: Essays on Victorian Fiction*, vol. 8, edited by Michael Timko, Fred Kaplan, and Edward Guiliano. New York: AMS Press, 1989. 1–17.

Kay, Lily E. *Who Wrote the Book of Life? A History of the Genetic Code*. Stanford: Stanford University Press, 2000.

Kearns, Katherine. *Nineteenth-Century Literary Realism: Through the Looking Glass*. Cambridge: Cambridge University Press, 1996.

Kermode, Frank. *The Genesis of Secrecy: On the Interpretation of Narrative*. Cambridge: Harvard University Press, 1979.

Kittler, Friedrich. "The World of the Symbolic." *Essays: Literature, Media, Information Systems*, edited and Introduction by John Johnston. Amsterdam: G + B Arts International, 1997. 130–46.

Kucich, John. *Excess and Restraint in the Novels of Charles Dickens*. Athens: University of Georgia Press, 1981.

Larkin, Maurice. *Man and Society in Nineteenth-Century Realism: Determinism and Literature*. Totowa, NJ: Rowman and Littlefield, 1977.

Lettis, Richard. *Dickens on Literature: A Continuing Study of His Aesthetic*. New York: AMS Press, 1990.

———. "The Names of David Copperfield." *Dickens Studies Annual: Essays on Victorian Fiction*, vol. 31, edited by Stanley Friedman, Edward Guiliano, Anne Humpherys, and Michael Timko. New York: AMS Press, 2002. 67–86.

Levine, George. *The Realistic Imagination: English Fiction from Frankenstein to Lady Chatterley*. Chicago: University of Chicago Press, 1981.

Lloyd, Tom. *Crises of Realism: Representing Experience in the British Novel, 1816–1910*. Lewisburg: Bucknell University Press, 1997.

Lonoff, Sue. *Wilkie Collins and His Victorian Readers: A Study in the Rhetoric of Authorship*. New York: AMS Press, 1982.

Lopes, José Manuel. *Foregrounded Description in Prose Fiction: Five Cross-Literary Studies*. Toronto: University of Toronto Press, 1995.

Lukács, George. *Essays on Realism*, edited and with an Introduction by Rodney Livingstone, translated by David Fernbach. Cambridge: MIT Press, 1981 [First German publication 1971].

Martens, Lorna. *The Diary Novel*. Cambridge: Harvard University Press, 1985.

Maxwell, Richard. *The Mysteries of Paris and London*. Charlottesville: University Press of Virginia, 1992.

McMaster, Juliet. *Dickens the Designer*. London: The Macmillan Press, 1987.

Meckier, Jerome. *Hidden Rivalries in Victorian Fiction: Dickens, Realism, and Revaluation.* Lexington: The University Press of Kentucky, 1987.

Metz, Nancy Aycock. "The Artistic Reclamation of Waste in *Our Mutual Friend.*" *Nineteenth-Century Fiction* 34 (1979): 59–72.

Meyer, Leonard B. "Meaning in Music and Information Theory." *Journal of Aesthetics and Art Criticism* (June 1957).

Miller, J. Hillis. *Charles Dickens: The World of His Novels.* Cambridge: Harvard University Press, 1965.

———. "Introduction." *Bleak House,* edited by Norman Page. Harmondsworth, Middlesex: Penguin Books, 1972. 11–34.

———. "*Sketches by Boz, Oliver Twist,* and Cruikshank's Illustrations." *Charles Dickens and George Cruikshank: Papers Read at a Clark Library Seminar on May 9, 1970 by J. Hillis Miller and David Borowitz,* Introduction by Ada B. Nisbet. Los Angeles: University of California Press, 1971. 1–69.

———. *Speech Acts in Literature.* Stanford: Stanford University Press, 2001.

———. *Versions of Pygmalion.* Cambridge: Harvard University Press, 1990.

Millgate, Jane. *Walter Scott: The Making of the Novelist.* Toronto: University of Toronto Press, 1984.

Morson, Gary Saul. *Narrative and Freedom: The Shadows of Time.* New Haven: Yale University Press, 1994.

Musselwhite, David. *Partings Welded Together: Politics and Desire in the Nineteenth-Century English Novel.* London and New York: Methuen, 1987.

Newcomb, Mildred. *The Imagined World of Charles Dickens.* Columbus: The Ohio State University Press, 1989.

Newman, John Henry. *Callista: A Tale of the Third Century.* London: Longmans, Green, 1904.

Norris, Christopher. *Truth and the Ethics of Criticism.* New York: Manchester University Press, 1994.

Phelan, James. "Present Tense Narration, Mimesis, the Narrative Norm, and the Positioning of the Reader in *Waiting for the Barbarians.*" *Understanding Narrative,* edited by James Phelan and Peter J. Rabinowitz. Columbus: The Ohio State University Press, 1994. 222–45.

———. "Redundant Telling, Preserving the Mimetic, and the Functions of Character Narration." *Narrative* 9, no. 2 (May 2001): 210–16.

Powell, S. D. "The Subject of David Copperfield's Renaming and the Limits of Fiction." *Dickens Studies Annual: Essays on Victorian Fiction,* vol. 31, edited by Stanley Friedman, Edward Guiliano, Anne Humpherys, and Michael Timko. New York: AMS Press, 2002. 47–66.

Prince, Gerald. *Narratology.* The Hague: Mouton, 1982.

Quirk, Randolph. *Charles Dickens and Appropriate Language.* Durham: Duke University Press, 1959.

Ragussis, Michael. "The Ghostly Signs of Bleak House." *Nineteenth-Century Fiction* 34, no. 3 (December 1979): 253–80.

Ramspeck, Beth Sutton. "A Photo's Worth a Dozen Novels? Mary Ward in the Turn-of-the-Century Gaze." Paper presented at the Midwest Victorian Studies Association Conference, Indiana University, April 27, 1996.

Reed, John R. *Victorian Will.* Athens: Ohio University Press, 1989.

Rimmon-Kenan, Shlomith. *Narrative Fiction: Contemporary Poetics.* London and New

York: Methuen, 1983.

Robbins, Bruce. *The Servant's Hand: English Fiction from Below.* New York: Columbia University Press, 1986.

Romano, John. *Dickens and Reality.* New York: Columbia University Press, 1978.

Ronen, Ruth. "Description, Narrative and Representation." *Narrative* 5, no. 3 (October 1997): 274–86.

Rorty, Richard. "Is There a Problem about Fictional Discourse?" *Consequences of Pragmatism (Essays: 1972–1980).* Minneapolis: University of Minnesota Press, 1982.

Said, Edward. *Orientalism.* New York: Vintage Books, 1979.

Schwartzbach, F. A. *Dickens and the City.* London: The Athlone Press, 1979.

Searle, John R. *Expression and Meaning: Studies in the Theory of Speech Acts.* Cambridge: Cambridge University Press, 1979

———. *Intentionality: An Essay in the Philosophy of Mind.* Cambridge: Cambridge University Press, 1983.

Shaw, Harry. *Narrating Reality: Austen, Scott, Eliot.* Ithaca: Cornell University Press, 1999.

Stern, J. P. *On Realism.* London and Boston: Routledge and Kegan Paul, 1973.

Sternberg, Meir. *Expositional Modes and Temporal Order in Fiction.* Baltimore: Johns Hopkins University Press, 1978.

———. *The Poetics of Biblical Narrative: Ideological Literature and the Drama of Reading.* Bloomington: Indiana University Press, 1985.

Stewart, Garrett, *Dickens and the Trials of Imagination.* Cambridge: Harvard University Press, 1974.

———. "Dickens and Language." *The Cambridge Companion to Charles Dickens,* edited by John O. Jordan. Cambridge: Cambridge University Press, 2001.

Stone, Harry. "What's in a Name: Fantasy and Calculation in Dickens." *Dickens Studies Annual: Essays on Victorian Fiction,* vol. 14, edited by Michael Timko, Fred Kaplan, and Edward Guiliano. New York: AMS Press, 1985. 191–204.

———, ed. *Dickens's Working Notes for His Novels.* Chicago: University of Chicago Press, 1987.

Sturgess, Philip J. M. *Narrativity: Theory and Practice.* Oxford: The Clarendon Press, 1992.

Sucksmith, Harvey Peter. *The Narrative Art of Charles Dickens: The Rhetoric of Sympathy and Irony in His Novels.* Oxford: The Clarendon Press, 1970.

Suleiman, Susan Rubin. "Redundancy and the 'Readable' Text." *Poetics Today: Theory and Analysis of Literature and Communication* 2, no. 3 (1980): 119–42.

Thoms, Peter. *Detection and Its Designs: Narrative and Power in 19th-Century Detective Fiction.* Athens: Ohio University Press, 1988.

Todorov, Tzvetan. *The Poetics of Prose,* translated by Richard Howard. Ithaca: Cornell University Press, 1977.

Van Ghent, Dorothy. "'The Dickens World: A View from Todgers's." *The Dickens Critics,* edited by George H. Ford and Lauriat Lane Jr. Ithaca: Cornell University Press, 1963. 213–32

Vargish, Thomas. *The Providential Aesthetic in Victorian Fiction.* Charlottesville: University Press of Virginia, 1985.

Villanueva, Darío. *Theories of Literary Realism,* translated by Mihai I. Spariosu and Santiago García-Castanón. Albany: State University of New York Press, 1997.

Watt, W. C. "As to Psychosemiotics." *The Semiotics of Culture and Language.* Volume

2: *Language and Other Semiotic Systems of Culture,* edited by Robin P. Fawcett, M. A. K. Halliday, Sydney M. Lamb, and Adam Makkai. London and Dover, NH: Francies Pinter Publishers, 1984.

Williams, Ioan. *The Realist Novel in England: A Study in Development.* Pittsburgh: The University of Pittsburgh Press, 1974.

Williams, Raymond. *The Country and the City.* New York: Oxford University Press, 1973

Winks, Robin W. *Modus Operandi: An Excursion into Detective Fiction.* Boston: David R. Godine, 1982.

Woolf, Virginia, "Mr. Bennett and Mrs. Brown." *Collected Essays,* vol. 1. London: The Hogarth Press, 1966. 319–37.

INDEX

Kingsley, Charles: *Alton Locke,* 15
Kittler, Friedrich, 116n4, 117n9
Kucich, John, 77

Lacan, Jaques, 116n4
Larkin, Maurice, 107n4
Lerner, Laurence, 107n6
Lettis, Richard, 52ff., 57, 113nn7–8,
    113n10, 115n3
Levine, George, 103, 116n3
Lewes, G. H., 1, 8
Lloyd, Tom, 90, 114n14, 117n11
Lonoff, Sue, 111n6
Lopes, José Manuel, 18, 110n12
Lukács, George, 3, 107n3

Mann, Thomas: *Doctor Faustus,* 58
Marryat, Captain Frederick, 44
Martens, Lorna, 33, 110n2, 111n8
Masson, David, 8, 107n1
Maxwell, Richard, 109n10
Mayhew, Henry, 15ff.
McMaster, Juliet, 114n13, 114n16, 114n1
Meckier, Jerome, 56ff.
metaphysical novel, 9ff.
Metz, Nancy Aycock, 115n5, 119n22
Meyer, Leonard B., 116n4
Miller, J. Hillis, 43ff., 57ff., 69, 75, 78ff.,
    83ff., 113n2, 114n12, 115n4, 115n7,
    115n2, 118n14
Millgate, Jane, 107n2
Morson, Gary Saul, 38ff., 112n22
Musselwhite, David, 57

names, 42–53, 113n1, 113nn3–5, 113–
    14nn8–17
Newcome, Mildred, 82
Newman, John Henry: *Callista,* 110n2
Norris, Christopher, 108n5

personification, 71–84
Phelan, James, 108n1, 112n20, 117n9
place in literature, 12ff., 17, 20ff., 52
Plato, 105

Powell, S. D., 113n1, 113n7, 113n9
Prince, Gerald, 27
Proust, Marcel: *Remembrance of Things
    Past,* 43ff., 113n2
providential narrative, 28ff., 40ff., 103, 106,
    111n5, 119n23

Quirk, Randolph, 111n4

Ragussis, Michael, 48ff.
Ramspeck, Beth Sutton, 110n14
realism, 1ff., 26, 42ff., 52, 56ff., 59ff., 69ff.,
    70ff., 85ff., 103ff., 105ff., 107n6, 115n6,
    114n17, 116n4, 116n3
Reed, John R., 116n5
Resnais, Alain, 111n14
Richardson, Samuel: *Clarissa,* 26
Rimmon-Kenan, Shlomith, 27, 112n16
Robbe-Grillet, Alain, 26, 111n14
Robbins, Bruce, 59
Romano, John, 57, 117n6, 119n23
Ronen, Ruth, 109n8
Rorty, Richard, 21

Said, Edward, 14
Schwarzbach, F. S., 109n7
Scott, Sir Walter, 1, 60, 107n2; *Bride of
    Lammermoor, The,* 1; *Rob Roy,* 25
Searle, John, 20ff., 110n15
Shaw, Harry E., 5ff., 59ff.
Stern, J. P., 1
Sternberg, Meir, 117n9
Stevenson, R. L.: *Treasure Island,* 25; *Kid-
    napped,* 25
Stewart, Garrett, 44ff., 75ff., 93
Stone, Harry, 46, 113nn3–4, 113n11,
    114n17
Sturgess, Philip J. M., 27
Sucksmith, Harvey Peter, 72
Suleiman, Susan Rubin, 117n7
Swift, Jonathan: *Gulliver's Travels,* 18,
    109n9

Tennyson, Alfred, 2